Christmas '96

Dear Ernie
    I know how our Papa loved
Charlie Chaplin, I hope you do too.
        Love
        Marge

The Life and Times of
CHARLIE CHAPLIN

The Life and Times of
CHARLIE CHAPLIN

Robyn Karney
and Robin Cross

SMITHMARK

This edition first published in 1992 by SMITHMARK Publishers Inc.,
112 Madison Avenue, New York, NY 10016

ISBN 0–8317–1251–1

Consultant editor: Robyn Karney

Design by Millions Design, London

Typeset by Cambrian Typesetters, Frimley, Surrey

Printed and bound in Hong Kong

SMITHMARK books are available for bulk purchases for sales promotion and
premium use. For details write or telephone the Manager of Special Sales,
SMITHMARK Publishers Inc., 112 Madison Avenue, New York, NY 10016.
(212) 532–6600.

Picture Credits and Acknowledgements

The publisher would like to thank the following:

Jane Burns and the Stills Department at the BFI

Gilbert Gibson
Aquarius Picture Library
(16, 17, 18, 26, 27, 29, 34, 36–7, 43, 47, 55, 59, 62, 68, 70, 71, 72, 78, 81, 82–3
[2 pictures], 87–8 [2 pictures], 93, 94–5 [2 pictures], 97, 104, 117)

Joel Finler Collection
(11, 28, 33, 46, 48, 64–5, 67, 74, 78, 86, 87, 95, 96–7, 103, 106, 112, 113, 116,
121)

Popperfoto
(9, 12, 13, 14, 15, 35, 40–1, 44–5, 49 [2 pictures], 84, 85, 99, 102, 110, 111, 114,
115, 119 [3 pictures])

CONTENTS

1   **THE KID**   *7*

2   **MAKING A LIVING**   *25*

3   **THE IMMIGRANT**   *41*

4   **THE TRAMP**   *53*

5   **THE CHAMPION**   *65*

6   **MODERN TIMES**   *89*

7   **CAUGHT IN THE RAIN**   *109*

FILMOGRAPHY   *124*

INDEX   *127*

THE KID

How does one account for genius? It's a word that is nowadays used too often and too easily for, in truth, the real genius is a rare creature, and everything points to the mysterious fact that the quality is born, not made. How else does one explain the undisputed genius of Charles Chaplin, fondly and familiarly known as Charlie throughout the world ('Charlot' in France)? Of course, the circumstance of a life plays its part in igniting the spark but, as we shall see in Chaplin's story, the spark is obviously present from the beginning.

OVERLEAF
Chaplin and Edna Purviance in The Tramp (1915) – the first of his films to employ the classic closing fade-out as the jaunty little vagrant, disappointed in love, skitters off into the distance, the screen closing in an iris on his retreating figure.

RIGHT
'Those big shoes are buttoned by fifty million eyes'. The Tramp, the single most familiar image of the century.

FAR RIGHT
The 12-year-old Chaplin, photographed in 1901, the year in which his father, Charles Chaplin Senior, died.

Charles Spencer Chaplin, named after his father, Charles Chaplin Senior, and his paternal grandfather, was born on Tuesday, 16 April, 1889, the son of music hall entertainers. The first year or two of the baby's life were unremarkable and, although his environment was working class, there was nothing to indicate the spiralling nightmare of insecurity, deprivation and hardship which lay in wait for him, but from which he emerged to become nothing less than a phenomenon of the entertainment world.

His particular and unique creative gifts co-existed with a character and temperament which embraced the invaluable assets of discipline, dedication, iron will and, most notably perhaps, obsessive perfectionism. The cockney slum boy whose schooling was, to say the very least, casual, was also blessed with intellectual capacity. In his adulthood, he became a voracious reader, not only of thrillers which he devoured for relaxation as so many serious-minded people do, but also of the writings of Freud, of books on history, philosophy and psychology. His natural vision and perception were enriched by his quest for knowledge.

It is no exaggeration to say that Chaplin was, by his early twenties, one of the world's most famous people. By one of those fortunate accidents of history, his rise coincided with that of the silent film, a form of artistic communication that was not inhibited by a language barrier. It was Chaplin's astonishing ability to convey character and emotion in mime, to touch a universal nerve beyond differences of custom, culture or nationality (with no more than a look or a gesture) that made him pre-eminent among his contemporaries. The wellsprings of laughter and tears are the same everywhere, and Charlie made everybody laugh and cry. He also

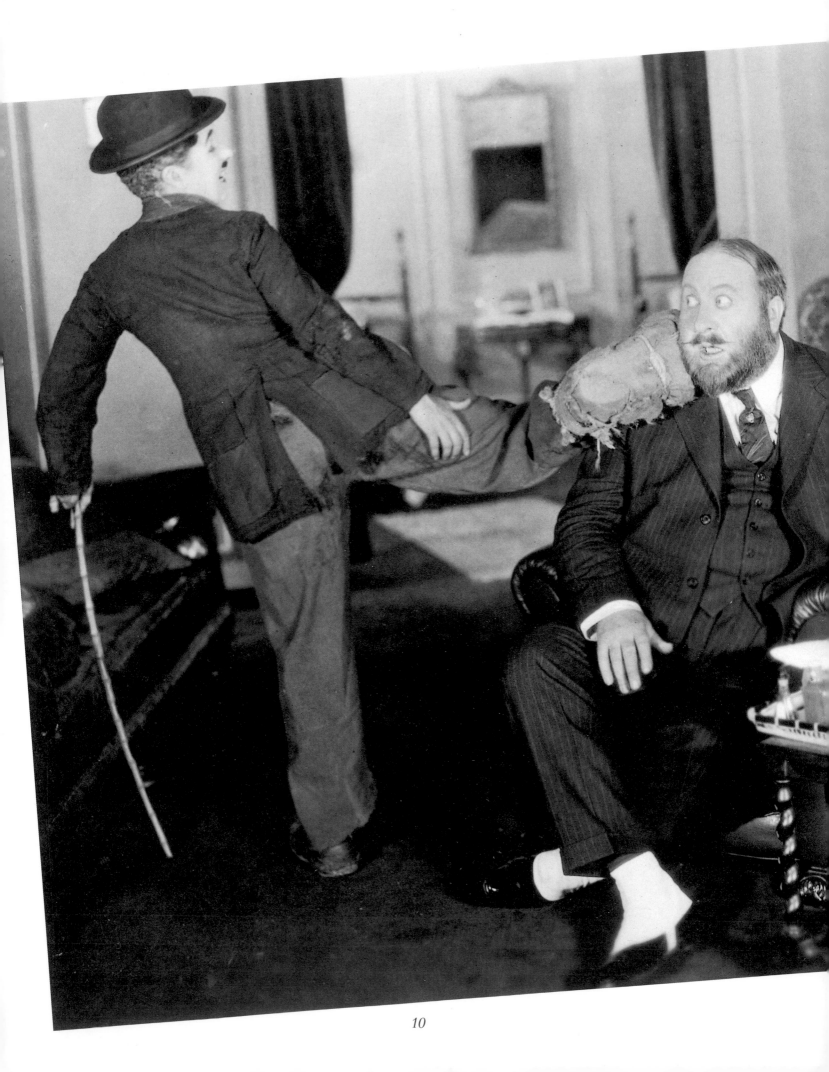

Chaplin as Adenoid Hynkel, absolute ruler of Tomania in The Great Dictator (1940). On the set Chaplin was dictatorial, creating a self-centred artistic universe in which only obedient mimicry was required from the faithful stock company who supported him.

LEFT
Buster Keaton, 'The Great Stone Face', at the height of his powers in the 1920s. Alcoholism and the arrival of sound destroyed his career.

brought a lasting contribution to the growth of film, being a daring innovator and a hard and unyielding taskmaster.

A hundred years after his birth, Charlie Chaplin is far from forgotten. In an age where fame comes and goes, new generations of movie lovers are encountering the 'Little Tramp' for the first time, and relishing masterpieces such as *The Gold Rush* and *The Great Dictator*. He has few competitors, the poker-faced Buster Keaton

LEFT
Chaplin pirouettes music-hall style in The Gold Rush (1925), reminding Mack Swain of the privations they endured in the frozen wastes of Alaska.

being perhaps the only serious challenger in the field of inspired silent comedy. Chaplin also ventured into the realm of serious film, his attempts at which are more widely appreciated now than at the time of their making. The honours heaped upon him before his death, the reconstruction of his films, and the hundreds of books which continue to be written about him, testify to his lasting fame. Humble Charlie, a millionaire before he was thirty, died as Sir Charles Chaplin in 1977, surrounded by luxury and familiar with the great and famous in every field. But the life that brought him adulation and riches had not always been thus.

FAR RIGHT
Chaplin the aviator, about to board an aircraft at Croydon airport, in north London, during his 1931 world tour. In Germany the Nazi press pilloried him as a 'Jewish' comedian from America.

OPPOSITE PAGE
Chaplin poses with Douglas Fairbanks at St Moritz, Christmas 1931.

RIGHT
Chaplin the musician. He had a natural musical talent but owed much to Fred Karno, who taught him how to use music to manipulate an audience's emotions.

London in the 1880s was a bustling, thriving city. Loyalty to the Queen and Country, and pride in the great British Empire prevailed. The industrial revolution and the rule of far-flung dominions had brought prosperity to the mother country, whose capital city was dignified and imposing. London was not yet scarred by the wars and technology of the twentieth century. Its handsome terraces and elegant squares, the impressive series of bridges arching over the Thames, the well-kept parks, the sweep of the Embankment and Parliament Square, created an image which inspired painters from Turner to Monet.

During the Victorian age, soon to yield to the softer grace of the Edwardian era, the aristocracy and the upper classes held sway in society. Stately homes were still places of private residence whose inhabitants took

their outside pleasures at the opera houses, concert halls, art galleries, smart restaurants and exclusive spas of Britain and Europe.

But, to borrow a phrase from Charles Dickens, it was the best of times, it was the worst of times. For there was another London, whose inhabitants were born without privilege, many of them forced to struggle for survival. For these people life was a grim affair. Admittedly, the worst excesses of the state-run institutions, which the novels of Dickens did so much to expose, had been eliminated by late Victorian times. Nonetheless, the shadow of the charity school, the

workhouse and the asylum loomed threateningly over
the lives of the poor for whom there was no alternative
when poverty turned into destitution.

The working classes of the time, however, combined
fortitude with good cheer and, whatever the hardships
experienced by the less fortunate among them, their
readiness to have a good time, their irrepressible
cockney humour, their energy and entrepreneurial gifts,
gave a vibrant quality to life in the streets where they
lived.

Often grey and depressing, these areas were enlivened
by the teeming markets where colourful hawkers shouted
their wares. There were public houses where rowdy
good humour reigned, and there were street entertainers
who, quite literally, sang for their supper, passing a hat
for pennies in exchange for a show of juggling or
dancing or fiddle-playing. It is perhaps no surprise that
the 1880s saw the rise of music hall as the most popular
form of mass entertainment. By the middle of the
decade it was entering its golden age.

There were thirty-six music halls in London alone,
among them the famous Alhambra, the ornate and
handsome London Pavilion (still standing) and The
Empire, Leicester Square, built in 1887 and now one of
the West End's premier modern cinemas. Throughout
the rest of Britain, well over two hundred music halls
opened their doors, the major provincial cities boasting
venues similar to their counterparts in the capital. The
ever-expanding public who filled them had to be kept
satisfied and the weekly change of bill saw a growing
demand for skilled performers.

The counterpart of vaudeville in America, the music
hall was really a sort of palace of varieties, presenting
singers, dancers, acrobats, jugglers, mimes, mimics and
comics. Many a gifted artist was nurtured on the circuit
– famous British stand-up comics such as Dan Leno, the
glamorous male impersonator Vesta Tilley, the legendary
Marie Lloyd. Several, in later years, went on to find
fame in another medium – a thin, morose looking comic

*Vesta Tilley, the legendary
male impersonator, whose
famous song, 'Burlington
Bertie', was an ironic
celebration of the life of a
London man-about-town.*

*Chaplin often played a
similarly fraudulent swell
when he was with the
Karno Company and in his
early days with Mack
Sennett at Keystone.*

Marie Lloyd, one of the greatest of music hall stars, who by sheer force of personality could transform the petty squalors of working-class life into a richly robust affirmation of life. Life wore Marie out and she died at the relatively young age of 52.

named Arthur Jefferson was to become internationally famous as Stan Laurel, one half of Laurel and Hardy – others enjoyed regular work and a good measure of popular support in the provinces, but were soon forgotten. What all of them shared was a certain level of proficiency without which they could not survive the competition.

It was this other London into which the most famous actor–comedian the world has yet known was born. If Charlie Chaplin's background condemned him to a childhood of deprivation and struggle, it also bequeathed him the environment of the music halls as a natural refuge from the harsh realities of life. It was in the halls that his genius took root, and was then disciplined, nurtured and refined. And it was in his experience and memories of the mean streets of south-east London that he would one day discover the fount of his creative inspiration.

Charlie was the son of Hannah Hill and Charles Chaplin Senior, both music hall entertainers who entered the profession in the mid-1880s. Hannah was the daughter of a humble bootmaker. She and her sister (Charlie's Aunt Kate) were both very attractive young women and, in 1884, the unmarried Hannah fell pregnant. It has never actually been known who the father was – Hannah herself somewhat fancifully claimed that she had run off for a time to South Africa with a certain Mr Hawke – but, on 16 March, 1885, she gave birth to a baby son, named him Sydney, and moved into lodgings with her own mother's former in-laws. Shortly afterwards, a pleasant-looking young man aged twenty-two called Charles Chaplin moved into the same lodgings.

Chaplin was the son of Spencer Chaplin, a butcher who later became the proprietor of a pub. Spencer's wife, Ellen, was a gypsy girl – the only ancestor of Charlie's who didn't come from straightforward English stock – and it's more than likely that the great artist inherited his distinctive jet-black hair and dark, soulful eyes from his paternal grandmother. On 22 June, 1885, Charles Chaplin married Hannah Hill. He gave his name to her baby son, who thus became the first Sydney Chaplin, the loyal and loving elder brother to the as-yet-unborn Charlie.

It was after their marriage that the newlyweds began their show-business careers. Kennington, the area in which they lived, was popular with many music hall artists, who used to gather at certain pubs in the district. Some of these watering holes provided lively entertainment for their customers, and it's more than probable that Hannah and Charles cut their professional teeth singing in such places.

By all accounts (most notably those of her famous son) Hannah was an outstandingly gifted mimic and a particularly shrewd observer of human behaviour. She doesn't appear to have capitalised on these gifts in her work; rather, she used them to entertain and enthral her

FAR LEFT
Chaplin's tragic mother Hannah, whose flair for observation and mimicry was absorbed by the young Charlie. Chaplin worshipped his mother, and her mental collapse was to find displaced expression in the crippled heroines of several of his finest films.

LEFT
A songsheet featuring Charles Chaplin Senior, a music hall artist of modest fame, who deserted his family and died of cirrhosis of the liver, a disease associated with alcoholism, in St Thomas' Hospital on 9 May 1901, only weeks after Charlie's last meeting with him.

small sons. The youngest son was particularly influenced by them, and displayed similar gifts himself in later years when he created his immortal gallery of silent screen characters.

Hannah's pretty singing voice and alluring appearance ensured a reasonably steady flow of engagements, which she filled under the stage name of Lily Harley. But, although she rubbed shoulders with some of the great names of the day such as Vesta Tilley and the young Marie Lloyd, she never climbed far above the bottom of the bill, and her full-time career proved short-lived. At the time of her life when she really needed the work, she was dogged by ill-health and by the onset of mental illness which was to haunt her for the rest of her life

and confine her to asylums for long stretches of time.

Her husband, however, fared substantially better. Charles was an adequate mimic and a stylish singer who soon took to specialising in the narrative ballads, both serious and comic, which were the staple musical diet of the day. His popularity grew, and was confirmed by the publication of his photograph on the sheet music of some of the numbers he helped to prominence. In addition, he composed a couple of successful songs himself, was always in work fairly high on the bill, and was therefore ensured an adequate living by the standards of the day.

But life for the music hall artist had its pitfalls. In order to keep working, they had to keep travelling, enduring endless train journeys across the country and

constant absences from home in often bleak surroundings. It was an unsettled and unsettling existence which took its toll. Many performers, often called upon to drink with the customers, embraced the good cheer of alcohol to excess – not to mention finding solace in amorous encounters. Unhappily, Charles Chaplin was to become one of the victims of this way of life.

When Hannah Chaplin gave birth to her second son at home in East Lane, Walworth, London, the baby's father was away playing at 'Professor' Leotard Bosco's Empire Palace of Varieties in Hull. Bosco was a colourful character in the profession and, many years later, Charlie Chaplin twice called a daffy screen character Professor Bosco, which indicates that his father must have told him stories about the original. In fact, throughout the years when he made his short silent films, Charlie drew on the names and habits of people remembered from his childhood to service his stories.

Thanks to Chaplin Senior's current success, the family moved into comfortable lodgings in West Square shortly after little Charles Spencer Chaplin was born. With its tall Georgian houses overlooking the customary central gardens, the elegance of West Square was, and still is, at curious odds with the otherwise humble and depressed area in which it is situated. Hannah was devoted to her boys and, although she returned to playing the halls from time to time, she would always leave them in the care of a reliable housemaid for the evening. Such was the relative affluence of the Chaplins, for a while at least.

In the late summer of 1890, Chaplin Senior was riding the crest of a professional wave and was offered a touring engagement in America which included a couple of months at the Union Square Theatre in New York. It seems that Charles and Hannah, no doubt due to their endless enforced separations, had been drifting apart for some time. Charles's long – and for him, enjoyable – absence in the United States effectively brought about the end of their marriage. Thus, before he was two years old, Charlie was fatherless. By the autumn of 1891, when the boy was two-and-a-half and his adoring half-brother Sydney six-and-a-half, their mother had formed a liaison with Leo Dryden, a music hall singer who had often appeared on the same bill as Charles Chaplin. Dryden was a handsome womaniser and a well-known figure in his own world, and Hannah found the flattery of his attentions irresistible.

The couple neither married nor lived together but, in August 1882, Hannah gave birth to yet another son and half-brother to Sydney and Charlie. The new baby was christened George Dryden Wheeler – his father's full name – and was much loved by his mother. But any happiness occasioned by his birth was short-lived. Six months later, Leo Dryden arrived at Hannah's home, snatched the baby away, and disappeared. This was the first of a series of catastrophes that were visited upon Hannah and her two remaining boys. At almost the same time, her mother, who had taken to drink and become increasingly eccentric and ill, was found wandering the streets of Lambeth and was carried off to the workhouse. In a matter of a couple of weeks, she was certified insane and committed to an asylum where she died a few years later.

Now without any visible means of support – Chaplin Senior was far from helpful in making any contribution to the welfare of his former family – Hannah took to doing odd nursing and dressmaking jobs for members of a local church congregation. This marked the beginning of a fervent religiosity in which she found comfort. She tried to resume her stage career, but her health was deteriorating and engagements were few. In 1894, however, she got herself a stint at the Canteen, Aldershot, which attracted a pretty rough audience comprised mainly of soldiers. She took Charlie with her. During the performance, the unfortunate woman who was in poor health, suddenly lost her voice, provoking a hostile reaction from the audience. The desperate stage manager, who had noticed Charlie doing little turns backstage, dragged the child on to replace his mother. With awesome aplomb, the pint-sized boy sang a comic cockney song, one of the hits of the day, entitled ' 'E Dunno Where 'E Are', to the evident satisfaction of the customers. This was the great Charlie Chaplin's first ever appearance on the stage, and his first taste of the rewards it could bring.

As David Robinson describes it, in his superbly written and detailed definitive autobiography, *Chaplin: His Life and Art*, 'The performance was a great success and to Charlie's delight the audience threw money on to the stage. His business sense was born that night: he

announced that he would resume the performance when he had retrieved the coins. This produced still greater appreciation and more money; and Chaplin continued to sing, dance and do impersonations until his mother carried him off into the wings.'

Chaplin, the future millionaire, was barely five years old. If the story of Charlie's first 'professional' encounter reads like a fairy tale, the circumstances which led to it were anything but. Hannah's ill-health grew worse and she was taken off to the Lambeth Infirmary for the first, but not the last, time. Worse was to come. Her mental state deteriorated and she was placed in the Cane Hill Asylum. She was never to be fully well again, although she became stable enough to live out her last years in Hollywood with her by-then-famous son. Throughout Sydney and Charlie's childhood and adolescence her sanity came and went. During periods of remission she would be discharged and was forced, with her boys, to seek refuge in the dreaded workhouse for a few days while seeking a humble room somewhere by way of a home for her little family.

The pattern was endlessly repeated. During her absences the boys, too, experienced the workhouse for brief periods before the Board of Guardians placed them in various charitable institutions. The only small compensation was that the boarding schools for the poor to which they were sent were reasonably well-kept and relatively enlightened. The Norwood School boasted a heated swimming pool and a pleasant rural setting. The Hanwell School in West London (to which they were transported in the back of a baker's horse and cart) offered a healthy regime and adequate food. Sydney was sent for merchant navy training to the *Exmouth*, moored in Essex, from this school.

This decision on the part of the authorities was to pay dividends. Sydney was diligent, made a success of it

LEFT
The Tramp seems a sly figure here, his lewd leer that of a satyr. The Tramp's overtures to women were ambiguous, sometimes tentative and sentimental, sometimes suggestive.

OVERLEAF
The Tramp cuts a series of capers which evoke Chaplin's music hall mentors. As ever, the cane takes on a life of its own.

and, a very few years later, put to sea for several journeys which resulted in money to help his poverty-stricken mother and struggling young brother. But the separation was hard on Charlie, who had grown very close to his brother, and who found himself entirely alone. Charles Chaplin Senior was now living with another woman by whom he had a child and, although ordered to contribute towards the maintenance of his sons, failed to do so.

This picture of unrelieved gloom for Charlie Chaplin, his mother and brother, continued for three-and-a-half years, from the middle of 1895 until almost the end of 1898. The details of the Chaplin comings and goings during this period would fill a small book in their own right. In order to give some idea of what the family were subjected to, it is worth recording a few known facts.

To take the last of these years, 1898, for example: on 18 January, 1898, Charlie was discharged from the Hanwell School where he had spent eighteen months, and his father was arrested for non-payment of maintenance. Two days later, Sydney was discharged from his training ship, and on 22 January, Charlie, Sydney and their mother were taken into the workhouse at Lambeth for a week before finding lodgings. At the end of July the boys were sent, not for the first time, to the

Norwood School, but by 12 August they were back in the Lambeth workhouse, from where they were discharged and readmitted in the space of twenty-four hours. Three days later, Charlie and Sydney were yet again sent off to Norwood. By 6 September Hannah was ill and in the Lambeth Infirmary, and by 15 September the hapless woman was admitted to the Cane Hill Asylum.

A week later, the Board of Guardians decided that Charles Chaplin Senior should take care of his sons and sent the boys to their father via a brief trip to the workhouse. The arrangement lasted only a couple of weeks. Chaplin Senior took little or no interest in his sons' welfare and the boys did not get on with their father's common-law wife who seemed to resent their presence. In November, Hannah was discharged from the Asylum and, on the face of it, the whole hideous farrago started all over again.

This time, however, a significant event took place. On 26 December, 1898, Charlie Chaplin opened at the Tivoli Theatre Manchester, as one of a popular clog-dancing troupe known as The Eight Lancashire Lads. Life for the family, although far from normal, would never be quite the same again. Charlie Chaplin, aged nine-and-a-half, had started out on the road to eventual stardom.

MAKING A LIVING

On 19 September, 1910, the Fred Karno company – the most famous, imaginative and successful troupe of entertainers in Britain – sailed for the United States to do an extended tour, beginning at the Colonial Theatre in New York. From there the company went on to perform in countless cities, major and minor, across the country. In was an arduous undertaking and a very successful one. The show attracted critical attention and large audiences. One of the most inventive and original members of the troupe was Charlie Chaplin, enjoying his first experience of the country which would later become his home and bring him fame and riches.

OVERLEAF
Chaplin with Henry Bergman in **The Circus** *(1928). He won a special Oscar for the film 'for versatility and genius in writing, acting, directing and producing', but did not reissue it until 1969.*

By the time the Karno company arrived in America, Chaplin was a hardened professional. His engagement with The Eight Lancashire Lads had plunged him into the rigours of the touring entertainer's life which was so familiar to his father. In Charlie's case, however, attempts had been made to see that he and the other boys in the youthful company were treated as children. He was sent to school – in Manchester, London and also for a spell at the school of St Francis Xavier in Liverpool. Wherever, in fact, the Lads were performing, they were packed off for their lessons, but it was an erratic education to say the least.

The Eight Lancashire Lads were, as the name suggests, eight young lads – except for the fact that, during Charlie's time with them, one was a girl with cropped hair. They were assembled and managed by a Mr William Jackson. He was a respectable married man and a devout Catholic, and his own sons were in the dance troupe. He knew Chaplin Senior who, it seems, persuaded him to take on Chaplin Junior. A deal was struck whereby the boy's board and lodgings were provided for, and the princely sum of two shillings and sixpence a week was given directly to Hannah. The newcomer was made to rehearse his clog dancing for six weeks before being allowed on stage; in later years he admitted to having been crippled with stage fright before his first appearance.

If the scope provided by the Lancashire Lads' routine was limited, it nonethelesss taught young Chaplin the rudiments of discipline and training in public perform-ance. A journalist writing in a popular music hall paper of the time said of their turn that it was 'a good one, because it gets away from the usual, and plunges boldly into the sea of novelty. The Lancashire Lads are fine specimens of boys and most picturesque do they look in their charming continental costumes . . .' Fine specimens and picturesque they might have been, but one of

Jackson's sons recalled that his first job when they took on Charlie 'was to take him to have his hair, which was hanging in matted curls about his shoulders, trimmed to a reasonable length.' Clearly, the dapper and beautifully groomed public figure of later years was, in childhood, a ragamuffin more akin to the Little Tramp.

Charlie stayed with The Eight Lancashire Lads through 1900. Their music hall routine was pleasantly and instructively interrupted by a stint at the newly opened London Hippodrome where they were engaged to appear as cats in the pantomime *Cinderella*. The famous French clown, Marceline, played Buttons, and Charlie was entranced as he watched him at work. Perhaps inspired by Marceline's imagination, Charlie made his own first excursion into improvised mime, giving his 'cat' some comic business involving a dog and a leg-raised-against-a-tree routine. The audience apparently was highly amused, the management was not, and the boy was forbidden to repeat his unasked-for contribution to the show.

At the end of the year, Charlie and the Jacksons parted company. It's not really known why, although some accounts have it that Hannah was unhappy about the arrangement, feeling her son was not well enough cared for. Whatever the reason, the budding young entertainer found himself out of a job and, with all ideas of school abandoned, facing an uncertain future. It was the beginning of two or three years of insecurity on all fronts, with Hannah's health veering this way and that and Sydney absent a good deal of the time. On 9 May, 1901, Charles Chaplin Senior died. Ironically, only a month or two earlier he had shown Charlie real affec-

LEFT
A standard signing photograph from Chaplin's early career. Fred Karno remarked of the nineteen-year-old Chaplin, 'He wasn't very likeable. I've known him go whole weeks without saying a word to anyone in the company'.

RIGHT
One of the Karno companies in their bus. A brilliant organiser with a genius for colourful publicity, Karno was a major force in turn-of-the-century music hall.

To little Mable
from Charlie

28

tion for the first time, and also seemed to be on good terms with Hannah once more. However, the debonair and handsome singer had been broken by drink. He collapsed with cirrhosis of the liver and dropsy, and was taken off to St Thomas's Hospital from where he never emerged alive. He was a mere thirty-seven years old.

His now half-orphaned son, living with the burden of an unstable mother, decided that the most immediate necessity of his young life was to earn money. He embarked on a series of jobs which were, if nothing else, dazzling in their variety. He began as a travelling flower seller, making the rounds of the pubs to peddle his blooms, but his mother so disapproved of this that he had to cut short the enterprise. Next, he found employment as a barber's boy and then he worked for a chandler. The chandler was succeeded by a doctor, in whose house he subsequently became a page, until he was sacked by the mistress of the house who failed to appreciate one of his inventive antics. He then went to work at W.H. Smith but, when they found out how old he was – or, to be more precise, how young – he was dismissed. He managed to survive a day in a glass factory before being taken on to feed the printing presses at Strakers the stationers, but that didn't last too long either.

Charlie fell back on his entrepreneurial instincts, and decided to emulate the street hawkers in his quest for pennies. Fired with enthusiasm, he set about it. In his own words, 'I ransacked the house for all the discarded garments I could find, hurried to the street and, mounting on a box, began in a thin, boyish voice to auction off my wares. The pedestrians stopped in amazement and watched me for a short time, and then, out of kindness, purchased my meagre stock. I returned home that night with a shilling and sixpence.'

After that brief foray into the world of commerce, he assisted a couple of men who made penny toys out of a miscellaneous collection of scrap materials. He admired

them immensely and soon decided to set himself up in a similar way, making toy boards. But the smell and the mess of the glue in their tiny lodgings upset Hannah, so the latest venture went the way of all the others. However, of all the things Charlie tried during those years, it was that one which seemed to have most meaning and, thirty years later, he told a friend, 'If I were to lose everything one day and not be able to work anymore, I would make toys.'

Such was Charlie Chaplin's life at the age of eleven (and twelve and thirteen). He was an energetic and enterprising urchin, with dreams of the stage, and only a sick mother by way of family. Then, in May of 1903, she became even sicker – gravely so – and was once more institutionalised. With Sydney away at sea, Charlie was left literally alone in the world and living – if one can call his bare existence that – by his wits and the occasional kindness of others. Fortunately, Sydney

SPECIAL ADDED ATTRACTION

Charlie CHAPLIN in "The Fireman"

NOW FUNNIER THAN EVER

REISSUED WITH MUSIC AND SOUND BY THE VAN BEUREN CORPORATION RKO came home from his seafaring voyage a couple of months later, intending to stay put permanently this time, and Charlie once more had the company, affection and strength of his older brother to see him through. The most significant aspect of Sydney's homecoming, though, was his announcement that he intended to pursue a career on the stage. Neither of them realised at the time that this decision would have far-reaching consequences for both their lives.

Fourteen-year-old Charles Chaplin now seemed to find a determination of spirit and a direction of ambition within himself. His mind made up to a life on the stage, he registered himself with H. Blackmore's well-known theatrical agency. It certainly took some nerve, and he was soon called in for an interview. Blackmore was impressed by the boy's presence and personality, and sent him to the offices of the legendary impresario, Charles Frohman (who later died in the sinking of the *Lusitania* in 1915). Again he made an impression, and Frohman's manager signed him to play Billy the page-boy in a new production of *Sherlock Holmes*, commencing in October and starring the distinguished actor and playwright, H. A. Saintsbury. The boy's salary was to be two pounds and ten shillings per week – undreamed of riches for one of his recent history.

   With some months to go before the start of rehearsals, Frohman's manager sent the boy to Saintsbury, who was casting a new play he had written. He, too, responded instantly to Chaplin's personality and immediately gave him the role of Sammy, a young cockney newsboy. This was not, as one might reasonably imagine, a mere walk-on or a line or two, but a substantial supporting role, and a comic one at that. In the event the play was a disaster, disliked by critics and public alike and forced to close prematurely. Charlie, however, in his first acting appearance, began as he would continue, and attracted his first critical attention as what the *Era* called 'a cheeky, honest, loyal, self-

The opening scene of The Champion, *an Essanay film released in March 1915. Charlie, now clearly a tramp, shares a sausage with a choosy pooch who won't tuck in until his food has been seasoned.*

reliant, philosophical street-Arab'. The paper also called him 'a broth of a boy' and felt he showed promise.

But it was the critic in *The Topical Times* who perceived that this youthful performer was no ordinary actor. Having mercilessly attacked the play (called *Jim, A Romance of Cockayne*), he ended by saying, 'There is one redeeming feature, the part of Sammy, a newspaper boy, a smart London street-Arab, much responsible for the comic part. Although hackneyed and old-fashioned, Sammy was made vastly amusing by Master Charles Chaplin, a bright and vigorous child actor. I have never heard of the boy before, but I hope to hear great things of him in the near future.'

As a result of the play's failure, *Sherlock Holmes* was moved forward. It opened in July, 1903, at the enormous (2650 seats) Pavilion Theatre in Whitechapel Road, before taking off on its countrywide tour. It was in these somewhat overwhelming surroundings that Charlie Chaplin played Billy for the first, but far from the last, time. He recreated the role three more times, and it was very good to him. In 1905, before his fourth and last tour with the play, part of it was given as an afterpiece to *Clarice*, which starred the distinguished actor William Gillette, at the Duke of York's Theatre in London's West End. Shortly afterwards, *Sherlock Holmes* replaced *Clarice* at the same theatre and at this point Charlie could well claim to be one of the privileged of his profession. He had come so far in such a short time that his new position in life put him in the way of a ticket to the exclusive occasion of the funeral of the illustrious actor-manager, Sir Henry Irving.

The youthful Chaplin gave the best part of three years to Conan Doyle's popular classic. When he finally stopped, the raw fourteen-year-old urchin had become a worldly-wise youth of seventeen, and he already displayed great financial acumen. Money, and the opportunities to make it, were never far from Chaplin's mind then and for the rest of his days. Significantly, given that the camera was to be the agent of his immortality, he bought one from his first week's wages – not, it must be said, from any artistic motive, but in order to earn extra as a part-time street photographer, a commonplace occupation in those days. It's also interesting to know that, when Charlie got his first part as Sammy, he was not yet able to read with any ease or fluency and, had he

had to sight-read for the role, he might never have been cast. But luck was on his side. He was taken on without audition, and it was the steadfast Sydney who coached him in the learning of the lines by repeatedly reading them to him.

Meanwhile, Sydney had a less successful time of it than his young brother. His longtime ambition to be an actor was as yet unfulfilled, and he took a job as a barman at the Coal Hole in the Strand. When, however, the role of the foreign Count Van Stalberg in *Sherlock Holmes* became available at the end of 1903, Charlie persuaded the management to hire Sydney and thus the brothers were together for the rest of that tour. During this time, Hannah had one of her temporary recoveries, and was released from the Cane Hill Asylum. She joined her boys on the tour. It was saddening for Charlie who was aware that Hannah had become the child and he and Sydney the parents. Although she shopped and cooked for her boys, she wasn't really relaxed and, after a month or so, decided to return to London. There her sons helped her to furnish lodgings and contributed to her upkeep, staying with her when they were themselves in the city.

Sydney wasn't needed for the 1904 tour of the play and went back to sea, sailing to Natal and back as an assistant steward and ship's bugler. His journey lasted three months, during which time he discovered and developed a gift for entertaining the passengers with solo comic turns. When he returned home, he decided his future lay in the music halls and he managed to find suitable work. From March 1905, Charlie was out of work, having finally parted company with Billy the pageboy. Unhappily, Hannah had been officially committed as a lunatic to Cane Hill, where she was to remain for many years.

In 1906, Sydney joined a company to tour a sketch called *Repairs*, about a bunch of comically inept workmen, and he managed to get Charlie in as the plumber's mate. The slapstick mayhem of the piece broadened the younger boy's experience and was later to serve, like so much else in these music hall years, as inspiration for some of his silent movies. During this time, Charlie answered an advertisement for boy comedians with a company called *Casey's Court Circus*. He was offered a job and he left the *Repairs* company. It was with *Casey's*

*Chaplin's brilliant
impersonation of the
celebrated hypnotist Dr
Walford Bodie. Charlie
scored a big hit with a
burlesque on Bodie while
touring with the Casey's
Court Circus Company in
1906. The Company's
manager Will Murray
recalled, '. . . he "got" the
audience right away with
"Dr" Bodie'.*

A rare photograph, probably of the Wal Pink routine 'Repairs', a burlesque on incompetent decorators, 'Messrs Spoiler and Messit', which opened at the Hippodrome, Southampton, on 19 March 1906. Chaplin is possibly the strange figure in the centre. There are echoes of 'Repairs' in his Essanay film Work (1915), in which he wrecks hapless Billy Armstrong's house.

a family in Kennington and led a rather undisciplined life for a while, trying unsuccessfully to work on an act as a stand-up comic. Meanwhile, Sydney had been taken on by Fred Karno's Silent Comedians and was proving to be one of their major attractions. Comedy sketches were the central ingredient of music hall entertainment in the early 1900s and, of all the well-known comedians who toured famous sketches, Karno's Silent Comedians reigned supreme.

Combining elements of mime, circus techniques and the slapstick comedy which was to find its fullest expression in silent movies with Mack Sennett's Keystone Cops, Karno's performers were the most versatile and talented around. He himself was an expert talent spotter and an imaginative man who specialised in wonderfully inventive theatrical effects. Under his personal direction, his troupe had so flourished that he had several companies, sometimes as many as ten, touring simultaneously throughout the British Isles and abroad.

During Charlie's period of unemployment, Sydney begged Karno to find his younger brother a job, but to no avail. Many months later, and with no particular enthusiasm, Karno agreed to give Charlie a two-week trial with the company and the boy got his chance in February 1908 at the Coliseum in St Martin's Lane, the largest theatre in London (now the home of the English National Opera). He was required to play the small part of a comic villain in a popular sketch called *The Football Match*, a role which normally served little purpose beyond setting up the entrance of the leading character.

However, amply demonstrating the stuff of which he was made, and to the surprise of the company, Chaplin turned the part into a comedy cameo. He made his entrance unconventionally with his back to the audience, dressed in silk topper and cloak and carrying a cane. Turning suddenly, he revealed a startlingly red nose in contrast to his elegant apparel and drew a big laugh. There followed a mime routine which elicited more laughter and involved tripping over his cane. Then, in the ensuing scene with the star of the show, he topped the actor's improvised quips with laugh lines of his own invention, to the discomfort of the other man and the delight of the audience. The Chaplin trademarks had been noticeably registered, and Charlie got his long-

that Chaplin's special gift for mimicry and burlesque really began to flower. He was given the star turns in the show and worked very hard to perfect them. He won much acclaim, particularly with his impersonation of a famous figure of the day called Dr Bodie who toured the halls as a self-proclaimed miracle doctor.

The job with *Casey's Court Circus* ended in mid-1907, leaving Charlie out of work once again. He lodged with sought-after contract. He was hired for two years, at a salary of three pounds and ten shillings a week, rising to four pounds in the second year, and with an option on his services for a third year. With Sydney earning four pounds a week, the brothers rented a comfortable flat in the Brixton Road and furnished it themselves, even managing a touch of exoticism in their choice of lamps and cushions. For the first time in their young lives, the Chaplin brothers were learning to enjoy security.

The years with Karno were of vital significance to Charles Chaplin's future. The ambitious and inventive nature of the company allowed him full scope to explore and develop his own comic creativity, and to perfect his extraordinary artistry in mime. This was his supreme gift – the ability to convey anything by deft gesture or by a look from those dark, expressive eyes. It was this quality the camera drew upon and which was to captivate future fans of silent cinema the world over.

The Karno period lasted for four years, long enough to see Charlie pass from late boyhood into young manhood, and it was during this time that he fell in love for the first time. It was in the summer of 1908 when he was nineteen that he met Henrietta Kelly, known as Hetty, a dancer in a company on the same bill as the Karno comapny at the Streatham Empire, London. He saw her from the wings and was instantly enchanted – a feeling that increased when she came off stage and asked him to hold up a mirror for her. He plucked up the courage to ask her out to supper that Sunday evening and, for the next three days, got up to meet her at seven every morning and walk her to the underground station on her way to rehearsals. Hetty however confessed that she felt herself too young to reciprocate Charlie's feelings. She went home from their meeting in tears and, although the smitten youth prevailed upon her mother to let him see her once more, she was cold and distant and the brief idyll was over.

Chaplin never forgot Hetty, writing of her in various memoirs over the years with poignant nostalgia. As his biographer, David Robinson, so acutely sums it up: 'For

Bohemian high jinks in **A Woman of Paris** *(1923), Chaplin's first for United Artists. A serious drama, it greatly influenced the style of Ernst Lubitsch.*

anyone else it would have been an adolescent infatuation, a temporary heartbreak forgotten in a week. But Chaplin was not like anyone else, and something in his sensibilities or rooted in the deprivation of his childhood caused this encounter to leave a deep and ineradicable impression upon him.'

Fortunately, work didn't leave too much time for nursing a broken heart, and the following autumn Charlie had his first trip to Paris, where the Karno troupe was engaged to play at no less a venue than the Folies Bergére. In spite of language barriers, he responded with pleasure and excitement to this elegant and graceful city. He would one day return as the revered and beloved 'Charlot' of the French, and the city was the backdrop for his first independent feature film for United Artists in 1923, *A Woman of Paris*. The trip was also of immediate professional importance, since it launched Charlie in one of Karno's most elaborate comic sketches, *Mumming Birds*, the piece which was to contribute substantially to his success in America.

Chaplin was maturing into a complex and contradictory man. There are many differing opinions and accounts of his behaviour and personality and there is no reason to doubt that most of them are true. Perhaps it was his many-faceted nature that fuelled his genius, and which has contributed to the world's continuing interest in him. It is worth noting just a few personal opinions of him recalled from the Karno days.

Stan Laurel, then a young comedian known as Stanley Jefferson, was also in the Karno company and he said of Charlie, 'To some of the company I know he appeared

Stan Laurel, one half of the immortal comedy pairing of Laurel and Hardy. As Stanley Jefferson he had created for the Karno Company the role of Jimmy the Fearless, which was later taken over by Chaplin. He accompanied Chaplin on the Karno tours of America in 1910 and 1912.

Casey's Court Circus
Company in 1906. Chaplin,
now a seasoned
professional and wearing
a bowler, sits on the right
of the proprietor Will
Murray. In 1921 Murray
reminisced about taking
Chaplin on: 'I put him
through his paces. He
sang, danced and did a
little of practically everything in the entertaining
line. He had the makings
of a "star" in him, and I
promptly took him on,
salary 30 shillings per
week'. Chaplin left Casey's
Court Circus in July 1907
at the end of their tour.

stand-offish and superior. He wasn't, he wasn't at all
. . . he is a very, very shy man. You could even say he
is a desperately shy man . . .'. To Fred Goodwins, a
vaudeville colleague who later worked a little in films
with him, Charlie was a dreamer, and also ambitious 'in
a peculiar way . . . he loves his success and fights hard
to retain it, but only because he feels it is his due'.
Goodwins also described him as very abstemious, with
no vices, and very thrifty but not mean. Contradictorily
he saw him as 'one of the lightest-hearted men I have
ever known', while remarking that he was very highly
strung and that 'a little incident . . . the merest mishap,
will crumple him up completely. Sympathy, light-
heartedness and his amazing commonsense are perhaps
his strongest characteristics.'

Fred Karno himself, in contrast to Mr Blackmore the
agent, Charles Frohman's management, and the distinguished H. A. Saintsbury, who were all so immediately
enchanted with him and set him on the road to success,
said, 'He wasn't very likeable. I've known him go
whole weeks without saying a word to anyone in the
company. Occasionally he would be quite chatty, but
on the whole he was dour and unsociable. He lived like
a monk, had a horror of drink, and put most of his
salary in the bank as soon as he got it.' But, whatever he
felt about his young star's personality, Karno had the
greatest respect for him and was only too well aware of
Chaplin's value to his company.

But whatever the truth about Chaplin the man,
Chaplin the artist, on his first arrival in America, was
unequivocally ready to embrace the great changes that
were steadily approaching.

THE IMMIGRANT

3

The destination of the *SS Cairnrona*, carrying the Fred Karno troupe, was Quebec. The company disembarked and continued their journey by train, via Toronto, to New York. Beginning at the Colonial Theatre, they spent about three months in and around New York State, enjoying a less ecstatic reception than they might have expected. The problem, apparently, was a new sketch called *The Wow Wows, or A Night In London Society*, which they had never performed before. Karno had insisted that they open with this piece, but the actors all thought it silly and un-funny – an opinion confirmed by the American critics.

Even in this relative failure however, the newscomer to the circuit found personal success. That bible of the country's show business industry, *Variety*, remarked that 'Chaplin will do alright for America, but it is too bad that he didn't first appear in New York with something more in it than this piece'; and a critic elsewhere wrote, 'Charles Chaplin is so arriving a comedian that Mr Karno will be forgiven for whatever else the act may lack'.

Matters improved on tour once the actors, with Chaplin doubtless making a major creative contribution, had worked at the sketch and built it up into something rather funnier than it had been at the beginning. Wherever they went, it was recognised that Charlie was an outstanding talent. Quite aside from professional considerations, the tour was an amazing introduction to America for the young cockney performer. They spent twenty-one months there in all, on the road apart from a six-week Christmas season back in New York at the American Music Hall.

It was a way of seeing the country that anybody would have envied – crossing the vast landscape from East to West by train, staying in major cities with everything arranged and paid for, meeting the locals, treated as celebrities, and all the time following one's chosen profession to warm acclaim. Among the many and contrasting places that Charlie visited in company with his fellow actors were Chicago, St Louis, Minneapolis, St Paul, Kansas City, Denver, Butte, Tacoma, Seattle, Portland, San Francisco and Los Angeles. Ironically, given that it would be the centre of

A poster for Karno's first tour of the United States. The portraits are, from the top, Amy Reeves, Alf Reeves, Chaplin, unknown, Chaplin and Stanley Jefferson, later to achieve screen stardom in his own right as Stan Laurel. A Night In A London Club was a 17-minute sketch which featured Chaplin in the familiar role of inebriated interloper.

his future empire, Charlie disliked Los Angeles. They also went to Canada, appearing in Winnipeg, heart of the wheat country, and in Vancouver. It was the critic in Butte, Montana – cowboy country – who called Charlie 'the world's greatest impersonator of inebriates and the biggest laughtermaker on the vaudeville stage'.

During his travels, Charlie continued to exhibit the manifold contradictions of his nature and personality. On the one hand, he found the New World exciting and

stimulating, loved the seeming classlessness of the society, and joined his friends and colleagues in having a really good time. On the other, he had periods when he was withdrawn and very serious-minded, indulging his gluttony for book knowledge in a quite awesome manner. He read philosophy and attempted to teach himself Greek (but even he had to give that one up after a little while). A journalist who interviewed him wrote, 'It is said of him that, when in a small town where he

could not secure a book to his liking, he purchased a Latin grammar and satisfied his peculiar mood for a time by devouring the dry contents as though it was a modern novel.' True or not, the anecdote is a telling one.

In his appearance, too, he was given to odd inconsistencies. Stan Laurel, who was Charlie's roommate on tour, gave the following description of him during that time: 'People through the years have talked about how eccentric he became. He was a very eccentric person *then*. He was very moody, and often very shabby in appearance. Then suddenly he would astonish us all by getting dressed to kill. It seemed that every once in a while he would get an urge to look very smart. At these times he would wear a derby hat (an expensive one), gloves, smart suit, fancy vest, two-tone side button shoes, and carry a cane.' Laurel also told how Chaplin 'carried his violin wherever he could. Had the strings reversed so he could play left-handed . . . He bought a

LEFT
Now one of the screen's biggest stars, Chaplin is at the centre of a Hollywood group in 1918. On his right is Ina Claire, a Broadway favourite and film actress whose second husband was the silent idol John Gilbert. Behind him are Sydney and Minnie Chaplin.

ABOVE
Poverty-stricken violinist Charlie serenades gypsy girl Edna Purviance in The Vagabond, *a Mutual film released on 10 July 1916. The film deftly combined sentimental drama and comedy of character, and established Chaplin as a film-maker of great skill.*

cello once and used to carry it around with him. At these times he would always dress like a musician, a long, fawn-coloured overcoat with green velvet cuffs and collar and a slouch hat.'

Clearly, the accoutrements of dress had developed a special significance to Charlie. When the Little Tramp came into being his clothes were no more nor less than a tattered replica of what a 'gentleman' of the time would wear. No doubt his background had ingrained into him the idea that a man's station in life could be identified and judged by his appearance. This is not an unusual observation in itself but, being Chaplin, it affected him profoundly and with memorable results. To this day he is instantly recognisable in even an abstract sketch that depicts his bowler hat and cane. Although, over the years, these have been the uniform of millions of city gents, taken out of context the image immediately suggests Charlie Chaplin.

The Karno company ended their long American sojourn in May 1912 after playing in Salt Lake City, Utah, home base of the Mormons. They arrived back in England in June and Charlie was met by Sydney who made the surprise announcement that he had got married. His wife, Minnie, was an actress with Karno and, since the marriage, Sydney had given up the flat that he and Charlie had so happily assembled and shared. It is impossible to know why loyal Sydney, who had always been concerned for his brother's well-being, should have done this without warning or consultation, but it is known that the news caused the younger Chaplin no small unhappiness. Their shared flat had been the first real security he had ever known and now he was once again without a home – shades of his unhappy past – and for the first time in their close and loving relationship there was a strain between Sydney and Charlie. As if that wasn't enough, Charlie also learned that his mother, still incarcerated at Cane Hill Asylum, was just as ill as when he had left almost two years previously. However, both brothers at least now had financial stability and they decided to spend some of their money on transferring Hannah to Peckham House, a private nursing home.

In the event, Charlie didn't have much time to feel deprived of a roof over his head, for Karno sent the newly returned troupe out on tour in England. By now,

the company were totally unified and expert at all they did, and the audiences at home loved them. But for all the warmth and familiarity of England, life seemed peculiarly dull after the constant excitements of America, and nobody was more pleased than Chaplin when Fred Karno announced that he had arranged a return visit across the Atlantic.

Another ocean voyage, this time on the SS Olympic sailing from Southampton on 2 October 1912, took a largely new assembly of Karno actors back to America. On the face of it, it was the same schedule as before, but this time life did not run on nearly as happily. The novelty of performing across the country – particularly as they were yet again saddled with The Wow Wows – had worn somewhat thin. Several unfortunate incidents occurred, including the troupe arriving in Butte, Montana only to discover that the theatre where they had played before had burnt down and that they would have to perform in a hall. Charlie was no longer enraptured with sightseeing, having had his fill on the first visit, and this time he was aware of a certain provincialism among audiences in far flung outposts of the country.

Nonetheless, he advanced another step on the road towards fulfilling his financial ambitions by acquiring a few oil shares. He was also, more importantly, bowling audiences over with his drunken man-about-town, the Inebriated Swell, in A Night in an English Music Hall. This was the new name given to the old sketch, Mumming Birds, already so popular in England and in Paris. In this sketch Charlie's talent for burlesque, knockabout and exaggerated politeness, assisted by top

hat, tails and cane, had reached a peak of perfection and drew the admiring attention of both critics and audiences. Disgruntled and bored he may have been, grinding out the same old material night after night, but it was thanks to the Inebriated Swell that his fortunes underwent a dramatic change.

In 1913 the movie industry was still in its infancy; sound was fifteen or so years away and full-length features were only gradually coming into being alongside the little one- and two-reel shorts which were churned out by the thousand and formed the staple stuff of cinema. When the early nickelodeons gave way to moving pictures, the pioneer movie makers worked mostly in New York, home of the famous Biograph Studios where D. W. Griffith made his mark. The technical facilities and know-how were primitive, the rate of shooting and editing breathtaking.

The first moves to California were made from about 1903 onwards. Certain film-makers went there to try and escape the restrictive trust laws governing production and distribution. Others went because they appreciated the light and the climate and the wide open spaces, and they saw the filmic possibilities of the landscape. Already, by 1913, the word Hollywood was synonymous with American movies although the place and its studios were a far cry from what they later became.

Early Hollywood was a curious mixture – a rather dusty, primitive and unsophisticated small town, surrounded by citrus farming country. The population of Los Angeles was small, the buildings one-storeyed affairs. As the movie colony grew, so did the legendary suburbs of Bel Air and Beverly Hills. By the early

LEFT
Douglas Fairbanks, Chaplin and Mary Pickford clown about on the set of Pollyanna *(1920). The movie was Pickford's first for United Artists and its huge success at the box-office firmly established UA.*

ABOVE
The founders of United Artists, Douglas Fairbanks, Mary Pickford, Chaplin and D.W. Griffith, take a photo call in January 1920. During the silent era United Artists gained both prestige and profits from the release of both its founders' films.

1920s, the stars already inhabited enormous and opulent homes built in a variety of styles ranging from Moorish palace to English stately home. The vast wealth that could be accumulated in these lax times before income tax laws were tightened up, combined with the out of the way atmosphere of the place, the curious working hours and the growing pressures of fame, seemed to spawn a degree of decadence among film people. By the early 1920s, scandal was rife – drugs, sex and even murder (the Roscoe 'Fatty' Arbuckle case perhaps the most famous of these), and the government felt it necessary to step in and appoint official arbiters of morality.

Among those few silent screen stars who achieved fame during the early 'Teens were Francis X. Bushman, Lon Chaney, the indomitable Lillian Gish (still working seventy five years later!), cowboy heroes William S. Hart and Tom Mix, Mary Pickford and Mabel Normand. Big names such as Garbo, John Barrymore, Gloria Swanson, Clara Bow and Gary Cooper followed a few years later as the industry, and the popularity of its products, grew – along with the development of the huge publicity machine designed to promote them as living legends. Waiting in the wings during the 'Teens were many comedy stars who would find fame and fortune in Hollywood during the roaring and scandalous

1920s, notably Buster Keaton, Harry Langdon, Harold Lloyd and Laurel and Hardy.

But in 1913 individual big names were few, especially in the comedy field where the pre-eminent force was Mack Sennett. The son of working-class Irish parents who had emigrated to Canada, Sennett had started life as a labourer before deciding to enter show business. He worked for several years as a minor performer in burlesque and as a chorus boy in New York until, seeing no real future for himself on the stage, he

ABOVE
Mabel Normand, a bewitching silent comedienne, whose popularity briefly rivalled Chaplin's. Scandal and drug addiction wrecked her career, however, and she died in 1930.

LEFT
Four founding fathers of Hollywood – Thomas Ince, Chaplin, Mack Sennett and D.W. Griffith. Ince died mysteriously in 1919.

RIGHT
Two contrasting stars of the silents. Inset, Lillian Gish, whose career began with D.W. Griffith in 1912 and stretched into the late 1980s. She was the perfect Griffith heroine, combining virginal purity and spiritual strength and starred in more of his films than any other actress. In the main picture Clara Bow, the 'It Girl' of the mid-1920s and Jazz Age symbol.

wheedled his way into New York's Biograph Studios as a supporting player, where he appeared in many shorts directed by D. W. Griffith. Described as a fun-loving rough diamond and a natural leader, he was gifted with comic intuition, and was hungry for knowledge about how films were made. He set himself to watch and learn from Griffith, and from technicians such as the great pioneer lighting cameraman, Billy Bitzer. By late 1910, Sennett was himself directing for Biograph, specialising in comedy, and it was there that he met Mabel Normand.

Pretty as a picture, Mabel Normand was considered to be one of the most gifted comediennes of the silent screen. She and Sennett formed a romantic liaison which lasted for several years, and it was as his leading lady in Hollywood that she reached the pinnacle of her success. Eventually, a rift developed between them and she joined not only the Goldwyn Studios but the Hollywood fast set. Her life there was touched by scandal – she was implicated in the mysterious murders of director William Desmond Taylor and millionaire Cortland S. Dines. She was rumoured to be on drugs, and with her career in the doldrums she died of TB and pneumonia at the tragically young age of thirty-six. But in 1913, these events were some years off, and Mabel's period of greatest success and happiness had just begun.

Two former bookmakers named Charles Baumann and Adam Kessel decided to go into the movie production business. They formed the New York Motion Picture Company, a parent to four subsidiaries, one of which was The Keystone Film Company, and invited Mack Sennett to join forces with them in 1912. The story goes – although there's no hard evidence to support it – that Sennett owed them a gambling debt and was forced to accept their suggestion as a way out of the problem. Whatever the facts of the matter, he left Biograph, went out to Hollywood and, as producer and director, headed up the new Keystone company. Mabel was his leading lady, and he had such well-known stalwarts as Ford Sterling, Mack Swain, Chester Conklin and the ill-fated comic, Fatty Arbuckle, among his regular company.

Keystone was soon acknowledged as the leader in the silent comedy field. As the film historian Ephraim Katz describes it, 'The typical Keystone product was a crudely constructed farce that derived its comic force not from the twists of a plot, but from a persistent succession of visual gags, a spirited, often vulgar, physical free-for-all that ridiculed anything and everything and merrily thumbed its nose at social conventions and institutions. Law and order were made a special target with the advent of the frantically incompetent Keystone Kops.'

Looking at Mack Sennett's background and the nature of his work, it's not difficult to spot that he has certain elements in common with Chaplin. It is certainly no surprise that Sennett was deeply impressed by Chaplin's comic virtuosity when he and Mabel went to see *A Night in an English Music Hall* at the American Theatre in New York. There are many differing accounts as to how Charlie Chaplin was invited to join Keystone as a silent movie comedian. It was certainly as a direct result

of the impression he made as the gentlemanly drunk in that sketch. Sennett claimed to be responsible, but so did several executives of the New York Motion Picture Company, and Adam Kessel himself was said to have seen the Karno show and spotted Chaplin's potential. The bottom line, however, was that, in May of 1913, Karno's company manager, Alf Reeves, received a telegram in Philadelphia where the company were playing, enquiring as to the whereabouts of a man 'named Chaffin . . . or something like that', and asking that such a person should communicate with their Broadway office.

Alf Reeves, realising that the telegram referred to Chaplin, passed on its contents and Charlie, totally ignorant as to who these people were or why they wanted to see him (he thought that perhaps his Aunt Kate had died and they were lawyers), went up to spend a day in New York for the purpose of talking to them. At the meeting all became clear and Chaplin, sick of life on the road, agreed to join Keystone. A contract was sent to Charlie in July, providing for him to start work on 1 November but, by the time the document had been back and forth for various alterations of terms, that date was changed to 16 December.

Not without a little regret and a certain degree of apprehension, but at the same time jubilant and excited, Charles Chaplin officially left the Fred Karno troupe in Kansas City, on 28 November 1913. It was an emotional leavetaking for the group had in effect been his family, and he and manager Alf Reeves were particularly sad to part. Karno himself was, of course, more than sorry to be losing the young man to whom he had taught so much and who had become his company's chief asset, but he made no difficulties and didn't attempt to stand in the young man's way.

Charles Chaplin, cockney urchin, arrived by train in Los Angeles in early December 1913 and installed himself in a room at the Great Northern Hotel. In his pocket was his contract with the Keystone Company engaging him 'as a moving picture actor' for one year at a salary of one-hundred-and-fifty dollars per week. He had never met Mack Sennett, and he had never set foot in a film studio. Within just one year he would have completed thirty-five films and become the favourite entertainer of a world at war.

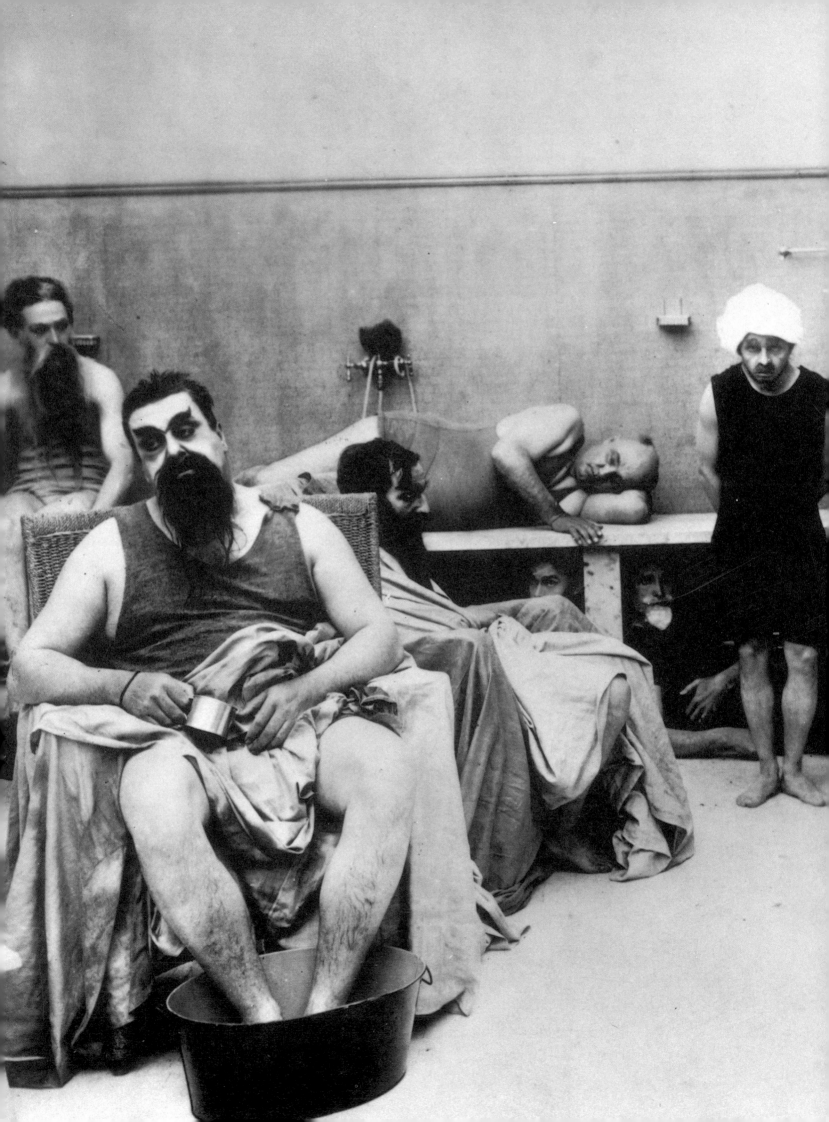

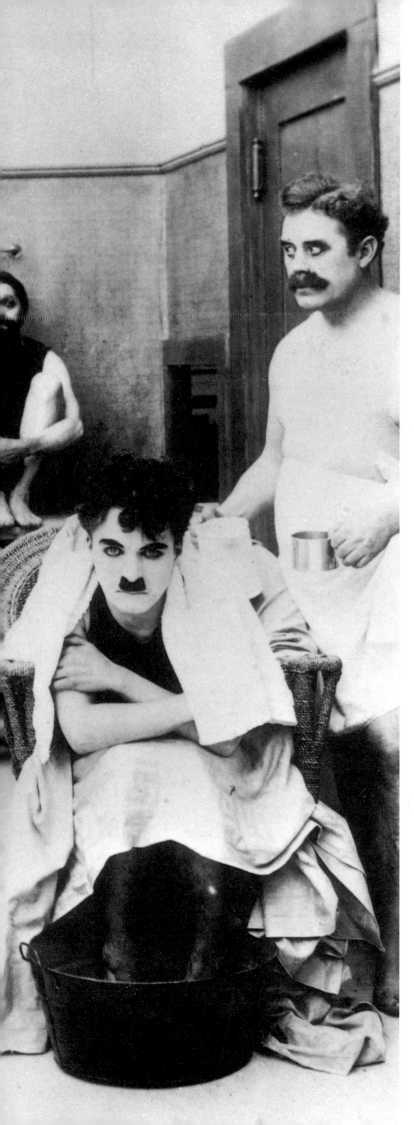

THE TRAMP

4

Chaplin's introduction to Keystone was not auspicious. On his first night in Los Angeles he went to the Empress Theatre, where he had played with Karno. At the Empress he bumped into Mack Sennett and Mabel Normand. Sennett was clearly taken aback by Chaplin's youthful appearance, but was assured by the nervous comedian that 'I can made up as old as you like'.

OVERLEAF
Eric Campbell (left) and Chaplin sweat it out in The Cure, *a Mutual film set in a hydro and released on Charlie's 28th birthday, 16 April 1917.*

Campbell, a magnificent heavyweight foil for Chaplin, died at the age of 37 in a car accident in Los Angeles on 20 December 1917.

According to Chaplin's autobiography, the next morning he travelled out to the Keystone studio, located in the run-down Edendale district, and was unnerved by what he beheld – a small ramshackle compound ringed by a green fence, its colourful inhabitants swarming towards their lunch when he arrived. Charlie turned on his heel and sought the safety of his hotel, only to be coaxed back by a telephone call from Sennett two days later.

If the studio was an alarming sight to the vaudevillian, so were its working methods. Films were assembled at breakneck speed with no time for retakes. Everything was grist to Sennett's mill: the dusty acres of nearby Westlake Park, the waterfront at Venice, public events, all were incorporated into the Keystone output which, for all its knockabout roughness, ran along efficient factory lines. Filming a one-reeler could take as little as a day and seldom more than four. A week later the negative would be ready for despatch to New York. From 15 December 1913, Sennett had undertaken to deliver three one-reel films a week plus one two-reeler per month.

Initially Chaplin was unsettled by the crude but effective pantomime language improvised by the Keystone players. It was the antithesis of the obsessive tinkering and polishing of the Karno routines. Moreover, although he was a vaudevillian of long standing and no little fame, in the movies he was a beginner, without experience as a film actor and yet to prove himself to his new colleagues. But he was to learn fast. According to his own account, he kicked his heels for a while at Keystone, absorbing the basics of film-making and making a number of small 'test films'. He made his debut in a one-reeler, *Making a Living* (released on 2 February 1914), monocled, moustachioed and fraudulently elegant as a flirtatious cad attempting to scoop eager-beaver reporter Henry Lehrman, who also directed film. No one was happy with the result and Charlie felt

that Lehrman, an unappealing Viennese-born hack, had sabotaged his best comic business. Nevertheless, the trade press spotted the newcomer: 'The clever actor who takes the part of a sharper . . . is a comedian of the first water'.

From the moment he stepped in front of the camera, Chaplin began creating sharply defined characters that revealed a sensibility which set him apart from the blur of crazy chases and flailing limbs which were the Sennett hallmarks. Chester Conklin, the walrus-whiskered comic who played second banana in some of Chaplin's early films, recalled that Charlie 'was a character comedian. He had to work slow. We got all our comedy out of fast movement, and Charlie couldn't do that.' As David Robinson has observed, Chaplin's work was distinguished by the inner resources he instinctively brought to bear: 'Keystone comedy was created from without; anecdotes and situations were explained in pantomime and gesture. Chaplin's comedy was created from within'.

The character of the Tramp – one of the most familiar images of the 20th century – emerged barely a month after *Making a Living*. His precise origins remain the subject of much scholarly debate, while Chaplin's own account in *My Autobiography* is tailored to fit the legend which grew up around him. Charlie recalled that the Tramp made his first appearance in a Mabel Normand vehicle, *Mabel's Strange Predicament* (released on 9 February 1914), in which he navigates tipsily through a hotel lobby and gets tangled up in the lead of Mabel's dog. He wrote, 'The day after I finished with Lehrman (on *Making a Living*) . . . I was in my street clothes and had nothing to do, so I stood where Sennett could see me. He was standing with Mabel, looking into a hotel lobby set, biting the end of a cigar. "We need some gags here," he said, then turned to me. "Put on a comedy make-up. Anything will do."

'I had no ideas of what make-up to put on. However, on the way to the wardrobe I thought I would dress in

RIGHT
John R. Freuler, President of the Mutual Film Corporation, presents an appreciative Chaplin with a $150,000 bonus.

Mutual's greatest claim to fame was the signing of Chaplin, who made some of his most brilliant films for the Corporation.

baggy pants, big shoes, a cane and a derby hat.' Chaplin's rehearsal gathered a crowd, 'not only the players of the other companies who had left their sets to watch us, but also the stage-hands, the carpenters and the wardrobe department. That indeed was a compliment . . . When it was over I knew I had made good.

'That evening I went home on the streetcar with one of the small bit-players. Said he, "Boy, you've started something; nobody ever got those kind of laughs on the set before, not even Ford Sterling . . ." .'

Although Chaplin improvised the Tramp into existence on the set built for *Mabel's Strange Predicament*, the character's first encounter with an audience outside the confines of the studio came a couple of days earlier.

At about 1.30 pm on Saturday, 10 January, the crowd which had gathered to watch a soap-box derby at Venice, then a small resort on the outskirts of L.A., were intrigued and then charmed by the antics of a shabby little spectator apparently determined to insert himself between a camera recording the event and the action. What had caught their attention was the filming of *Kid Auto Races at Venice, California* (released two days before *Mabel's Strange Predicament*), and the source of all the trouble was Charlie's Tramp. In his autobiography, the star fails even to mention *Kid Auto Races*, as it's generally called. Chaplin's subsequent silence on this typical Keystone exploitation of a public event may lie in the fact that, at the time, he might have believed that this was just another frustrating costume test under the direction of the disagreeable Lehrman, for whom he had conceived a heartly dislike; or that the exercise – mugging away in front of a crowd – was an insult to his talent. Thus, when he came to write his memoirs, he compressed his first experiment with the Tramp persona, developed on the set built for *Mabel's Strange Predicament*, with his actual performance in the film, which was almost certainly shot after *Kid Auto Races*.

In a remarkable piece of sleuthing, film historian Bo Berglund has compared the recollections of the principals in the story with detailed contemporary weather records

ABOVE
Chaplin, Harry McCoy and Mabel Normand in Mabel's Strange Predicament, *released on 9 February 1914, the film in which he later stated that he wore the Tramp's costume for the first time.*

RIGHT
The most famous rear view in the movies, instantly recognisable to children today. In his first public appearance the Tramp confronts a curious crowd during the filming of **Kid Auto Races.**

THE TRAMP

of the Los Angeles area – crucial in determining when filming was possible – to offer a solution to the mystery of the Tramp's origins. Certainly, the 'birth' of the famous little creature is more easily accommodated as a sudden inspiration on the Sennett lot, applauded by previously sceptical studio workers, than as the scrappy, snatched efforts at Venice, which ended up on a split reel with an 'interest' film, *Olives and Their Oil*.

History, however, has lent fascination to *Kid Auto Races at Venice*. For here is the century's most famous invented personality appearing for the first time, not in the artificial world of the film studio but in real life, twiddling and twirling his little cane and nervously doffing his battered bowler to an angry official as documentary reality grins and surges behind him. As Bo Berglund has commented, 'Fact and fiction are inseparably united . . . It is much as if, in the famous newsreels showing Queen Victoria's funeral, we suddenly identified Sherlock Holmes standing among the spectators.'

Keystone probably invented the legend that the Tramp's costume was assembled from the clutter of clothes left in the studio's communal male dressing room by some of Sennett's principal players. There were Roscoe 'Fatty' Arbuckle's voluminous trousers, pint-sized Charles Avery's tiny jacket, Ford Sterling's huge shoes, and a toothbrush moustache used by Keystone's favourite 'heavy', Mack Swain. The ensemble was completed by a derby hat belonging to Arbuckle's father-in-law, and the cane, supreme symbol of the Tramp's pathetic pretensions to the status of a swell.

In his autobiography, Chaplin merely records that he quickly devised the outfit as a contrast of opposites but, as we've already remarked, he drew on the deep wellsprings of his own past for inspiration. The Tramp recalls the costumes he wore in some of his music-hall routines: as a rag-and-bone man in 'London Suburbia', and as a slapstick decorator in 'Repairs' (of which a blurred photograph survives). There's something, too, of comedian Dan Leno in the Tramp's wistful manner. Charlie claimed to have modelled the skittering walk on the shuffling gait of an old Lambeth horse-handler named 'Rummy' Binks. But the Tramp's trademark technique of rounding a corner, pivoting on one leg

with the other revolving at the horizontal in anticipation of an abrupt change of direction, perhaps owed more to the 'funny walks' perfected by the Karno company.

Chaplin later claimed that the Tramp emerged 'fully formed' but, in fact, he was to tinker with his outline, developing and perfecting it for some years to come. What *was* immediately evident was the novelty of the character. Cameraman Hans Koenekamp, who photographed *Mabel's Strange Predicament*, recalled many years later, 'Did it look funny there and then? Yes, it did. Well, because it was *fresh* . . . and his movements, too. Wiggle the mouth and that moustache would kinda work. And the cane flapping around . . . and going round on one leg like he was skating'.

Although the Tramp of *Kid Auto Races* is caught in a characteristic Sennett knockabout, there is something about him which already marks him out from the Keystone ensemble. He seems to insinuate himself into the audience's mind. As the camera-struck bystander he

establishes himself as one of the audience watching the film itself – the great mass of people who hankered after getting into the movies but who, like the little Tramp, are always going to be chased away. Charlie's extra-ordinary ability to charm the audience is there in embryonic form.

But the Tramp had not yet established himself. In *His Favourite Pastime* (his seventh film at Keystone, released on 16 March), Chaplin played a comic drunk; and in *Mabel at the Wheel* (his tenth, released on 18 April) he was cast as a motorcycling villain in silk hat and frock coat. Mabel Normand had a hand in directing the film and fell foul of the obsessive pursuit of perfection which

was to characterise the rest of Chaplin's career. When she ignored his suggestion for a piece of business, he went on a sit-down strike. Charlie later reflected that, although he liked Mabel, 'this was my *work*'. In the future, absolutely everything in life was to take second place to his profession. This was sometimes detrimental to personal happiness and was certainly detrimental to the happiness of others such as wives and mistresses, who were involved with him.

Chaplin's chance to direct himself came with his 13th film, *Caught in the Rain*, which Sennett only allowed him to make after he had put up a $1500 guarantee against loss. A cheerful comedy of errors involving Charlie as a tipsy Lothario menacing Mack Swain and Alice Davenport as a husband and wife whose lives he reduces to a shambles, the film was an impressive directing debut. Chaplin had clearly absorbed much of D. W. Griffith's shot-by-shot tech-

nique, and the single reel contains more single shots than the average Keystone production. The standard set-ups, which included a park bench, hotel lobby and rooms on each side of a hallway, are handled with verve and attention to detail. As *Caught in the Rain* moves towards its climax, the titles fall away and a fluid succession of comic images takes over until the Keystone Kops make a typically chaotic intervention which leaves Charlie, Alice and Mack in a state of complete collapse.

By the time Chaplin came to make *The New Janitor* (released on 24 September and his 27th production for the studio) his grasp of film narrative and editing had progressed far beyond the amiable pell-mell of the Keytone product. Character and gags are integrated into the storyline, and there is both cutting between parallel action to maintain suspense, and a number of long takes which enable the comedy to develop. Even so, the

customary Keystone economies had to be observed: at the beginning of *The New Janitor*, for example, Chaplin (playing the eponymous menial) hangs his hat on an office hall-stand. It promptly falls off, and he gives it a distracted back-kick. This was almost certainly an accident, but retakes were frowned on at Keystone.

As early as June 1914, when he made a two-minute cameo appearance as a balletic boxing referee in *The Knockout*, the English newcomer's popularity was already sufficient for his name to appear above the title. A large part of *Mabel's Busy Day* (his 18th film at Keystone) was filmed at a racetrack. Much had changed since *Kid Auto Races* where the milling throng had initially assumed that Charlie was a fellow spectator. Now his very presence at an event swelled the crowd, which had to be roped off from the cast and crew.

The breakthrough to a wide public came with the well-known *Tillie's Punctured Romance*, directed by Mack Sennett and released on 14 November. This was the first full-length comedy feature film, a six-reeler starring the famous Marie Dressler in an adaptation of her stage hit, *Tillie's Nightmare*. It was the only time since becoming established in his screen career that Chaplin played second fiddle to another star. It was also the last film in which he appeared in a major role under the direction of somebody other than himself. Chaplin was cast as a dapper, citified conman, alternately

pursuing his former sweetheart, pretty Mabel Normand and Dressler, a bulky farm girl who has suddenly become rich. This time Sennett spared no expense and shooting lasted for fourteen weeks. *Tillie's Punctured Romance* was a big hit for Dressler, but its success owed much to the playing of her two co-stars, and subsequent attempts to repeat the formula without them in *Tillie's Tomato Surprise* (1915) and *Tillie Wakes Up* (1917), failed at the box-office.

Chaplin's thirty-fifth and last film for Keystone was *His Prehistoric Past*, a burlesque of Griffith's *Man's Genesis* (1912). It was released almost exactly ten months after his first, *Making a Living*. Charlie Chaplin was indeed now making a healthy living from the movies at $175 per week, but this hardly reflected his box-office value to Mack Sennett. When his contract came up for renewal, Chaplin demanded $1000 a week. Sennett replied with a counter-offer of a three-year contract at $500 a week in the first year, rising to $1500 in the third, but Chaplin felt that it was time to move on from the Sennett lot. For all its limitations Keystone had helped him climb the nursery slopes of the movie business but now, as an established comic star, he wanted to spread his wings and meet new challenges.

LEFT
'He ain't no good for either of us'. Conman Charlie, Marie Dressler and Mabel Normand in Tillie's Punctured Romance *(1916), shot over 14 weeks and the first feature-length comedy film.*

RIGHT
Caveman Charlie, complete with battered bowler, in His Prehistoric Past, *released on 7 December 1914, and his last for Keystone. Burlesquing D.W. Griffith's* Man's Genesis *(1912), the Tramp falls asleep on a park bench and dreams of prehistoric romance.*

THE CHAMPION 5

Billed as nothing less than 'The World's Greatest Comedian', Charlie Chaplin moved to Essanay at a salary of $1250 a week. Essanay, a production and distribution company, had been founded in Chicago in 1907 by George K. Spoor and the cowboy star G. M. 'Broncho Billy' Anderson. Its name derived from the first letters of the partners' surnames, 'S' and 'A'. Specialising in Westerns and comedies (it styled itself 'The House of Comedy Hits'), Essanay had already fostered the talents of Wallace Beery, Ben Turpin, Max Linder, and one of the first great romantic heroes of the screen, Francis X. Bushman.

OVERLEAF

In the ring in City Lights
*(1931), the most brilliant
of the many boxing
scenes in Chaplin's films.
Caught up in the action
are Allan Garcia (left) and
Fred Mann. Central to*

*Chaplin's comedy was an
athleticism and grace
which he had acquired in
his music hall days and
which he kept well into
his seventies.*

Chaplin made his first Essanay film in the company's Chicago studio. Released on 1 February 1915, *His New Job* was conveniently set in the studio itself, where Charlie wreaks havoc, giggling behind his hand as the destruction mounts, and applying a nifty boot to the backside of anyone who attempts to intervene. Making her screen debut in a small part as a stenographer was Gloria Swanson. Chaplin had tested her for a larger role in the film, but the determined Gloria, whose ambition was to be a dramatic actress, was deliberately uncooperative. The Chicago set-up was not to Chaplin's liking, and his feathers were ruffled by a brush with the imperious head of the scenario department, one Louella Parsons, who later became Hearst Newspapers' much feared and poisonous gossip columnist. The remainder of Charlie's Essanay films were made in California, at the company's Niles Studio and at the former Majestic Studio.

In the first movie made at Niles, *A Night Out*, Chaplin and cross-eyed little Ben Turpin played a couple of drunks whose attempts to appear sober and dignified leave mayhem in their wake. The pairing with the diminutive Turpin, master of misplaced braggadocio, was a happy one. Of greater significance, however, was the debut in *A Night Out* of a pretty, twenty-year-old blonde named Edna Purviance. Edna was to be Charlie's leading lady in thirty-five films over the next eight years, and remained on his payroll until her death in 1958.

Meanwhile, the Tramp was still developing. *In the Park* (released on 18 March), a throwback to the Keystone 'park' films, revealed the sly, violent side of his character. He picked pockets, stunned Edna's beau (Bud Jamison) with a brick before using the unfortunate man's gaping mouth as an ashtray, and pulled hideous faces while Edna's back was turned. When she kisses

LEFT
A bleary Ben Turpin and Charlie toast Leo White in A Night Out, *released on 15 February 1915. Although Chaplin's screen pairing with Turpin worked well, the two men disliked each other. Turpin, later a star with Mack Sennett, considered Chaplin a snob off the set and an autocrat on it.*

BELOW
Edna Purviance, the first and most durable of Chaplin's young 'discoveries'. A San Francisco secretary, she was picked by Chaplin to succeed Mabel Normand and starred in nearly all his films until 1923. She remained on his payroll till her death in 1958.

him, however, he careers wildly across the landscape in a mad dance which anticipates Charlie's cavortings in *Sunnyside* and *Modern Times*.

The Tramp's romantic yearnings emerged in *A Jitney Elopement* (released on 1 April) and *The Tramp* (11 April). In the latter, audiences were treated to the first of the trademark fade-outs in which Charlie's shabby, indomitable little figure – now clearly identified as a tramp – toddles away into the distance, disappointed in love but jauntily facing the future, fostering our own sense of loss and a hope that he will soon return. From the outset, Chaplin's uncanny ability to charm an audience and to indulge its fantasies was unequalled in silent cinema.

The tenderness of the Tramp's feelings towards Edna on the screen was a reflection of Chaplin's relationship with the lovely actress off the set. Some charming notes and letters which they sent to each other during this period have survived, and the terms of endearment in which they are couched suggest that Chaplin and Purviance were more than just good friends.

After *By the Sea* (released on 29 April), a slapstick romp shot in a day on a seafront round Crystal Pier, the director-star was allowed to take more time and trouble over his films. Subsequently only one Chaplin production appeared per month. In *Work* he played an exploited decorator whose attempts to refurbish peppery Bill Armstrong's home produce a colossal climactic

Edna Purviance, Charlie and 'Scraps' in A Dog's Life, **a First National film released on 14 April 1918. 'Scraps', whose real name** was Mutt, adored Charlie and pined away and died in his absence. He was buried in the studio grounds.

ABOVE
Charlie, Edna and Leo White in A Jitney Elopement, *in which the Tramp posed as Count Chloride de Lime to win the fair Edna's hand. Leo White, an Englishman who specialised in playing peppery Continentals, was the real Count.*

RIGHT
Chaplin in fetching drag in A Woman, *released on 12 July 1915. His skill as a female impersonator, and the slightly risqué tone of the film, which included some saucy business with a naked statuette and lampshade, led to a Scandinavian ban.*

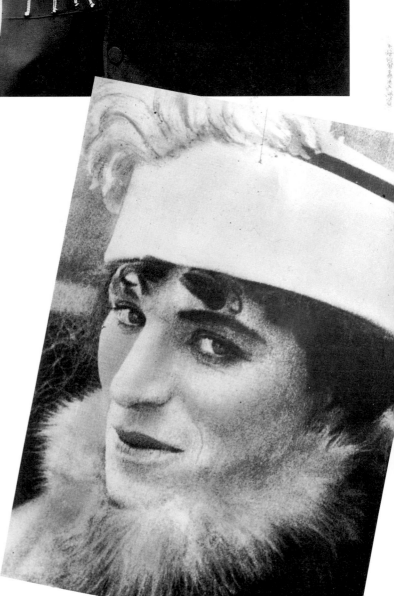

explosion which buries all the principals under a mountain of rubble. *A Woman* provided him with the opportunity to disappear into drag. (At Keystone he had appeared as a woman twice: once as a working-class termagant in *A Busy Day* and then as a society lady in *The Masqueraders*). In *A Woman* he appears as a sophisticated lady of fashion whose clothes are suddenly rearranged to form a clown's outfit. Chaplin's easy assumption of a convincingly female grace is both exquisite and mildly disturbing (something that might shame a woman with its refinement.) It is a pheno-

A sound era poster for The Bank, *originally released on 9 August 1915 and one of Chaplin's most accomplished comedies. As a bank janitor with an unrequited love for Edna Purviance, Chaplin injected a note of tragi-comedy entirely new to the movies.*

menon which prompted the critic David Thomson to observed that 'the history of bisexuality in the movies began with Chaplin, and the impression of sophistication that he gave in his earliest work is less a quality of the films than his own Cherubino-like refinement amid so much mugging'.

The most popular as well as the most accomplished of Chaplin's films with Essanay was *The Bank*, which opened with one of his most memorable gags. Descending into the bowels of a huge city bank, Charlie struggles to open an imposing safe whose door finally swings open to reveal a pail, a mop and a janitor's uniform. Much of *Shanghaied* was filmed aboard a real ship, the 'Vaquero', and the rest in a cabin built on rockers which created an authentic sense of the stomach-churning perils of the deep (echoes of which are to be found over fifty years later in *A Countess from Hong Kong*). *A Night in the Show* was an adaptation of the

TOP
Charlie creates a new line in The Floorwalker, released on 15 May 1916. Albert Austin and Leo White observe.

LEFT
Music-hall slapstick with Charles Insley in Work.

BELOW
Chaplin's elegantly inebriated Mr Pest makes up to May White in A Night in the Show, released on 20 November 1915, a throwback to his Karno days and the sketches of the American tours of 1910 and 1912.

old Fred Karno hit sketch, *Mumming Birds*. Charlie took the dual role of the drunken theatre-going toff Mr Pest, and Mr Rowdy, an equally inebriated member of the great unwashed in the gallery, pelting the stalls with rotten tomatoes and perpetually threatening to plunge from his unsteady perch.

Charlie Chaplin's Burlesque on Carmen – expanded from two reels to four without his permission after he left the studio – was Charlie's last film at Essanay, released on 22 April 1916. It was a clumsy send-up of Cecil B. DeMille's *Carmen*, with Chaplin prancing around as 'Darn Hosiery'. When he saw the finished version he took to his bed for two days in disgust. He subsequently sued Essanay unsuccessfully over the film, but resisted the temptation to sue again when, in 1918, the company cobbled together a two-reeler, *Triple Trouble*, from unused Chaplin material.

Chaplin's popularity had now reached such a point that the Chicago journalist Gene Morgan could write of the Tramp: 'Those big shoes are buttoned by fifty million eyes'. The star himself began to experience the heavy pressures of celebrity. On a trip to New York in February 1916 he had to leave his train at 125th Street station in order to avoid the huge crowd which had gathered to greet him at Grand Central. The Tramp was assuming a life of his own in Chaplin look-alike contests, comic strips, books, and a series of animated cartoons. Songs about Charlie, or 'Charlot' as he was known in France, proliferated. Among them was one written by the British comedian Lupino Lane. It was called 'Watch Your Step' and ran:

Since Charlie Chaplin became all the craze,
Everyone copies his funny old ways;
They copy his hat and the curl in his hair,
His moustache is something you cannot compare.
They copy the ways he makes love to his girls,
His method is a treat;
There's one thing about Charlie they never will get,
And that is the shoes on his feet.

Nevertheless, there were many professional Chaplin imitators. They included an old Karno colleague, Billie Ritchie, who appeared in a number of films made by the unprincipled Lehrman's L-KO company. There was also Billy West, who appeared in about fifty one- and

two-reelers in which he played a character very similar to the Tramp, which he claimed to have originated in vaudeville; and another Karno alumnus, Stanley Jefferson (later Stan Laurel) who was doing a Chaplin act in vaudeville. Charlie chose to ignore his imitators, although in 1917 he did launch lawsuits against some of the more flagrant offenders.

Plagiarism on this scale was a kind of flattery, but more welcome perhaps was an article written by the distinguished stage actress Minnie Maddern Fiske and published in *Harper's Weekly* on 6 May 1916, under the title 'The Art of Charles Chaplin'. Its subject could now bask in the intellectual respectability conferred by people who usually considered the movies merely vulgar fare for the masses.

For one so celebrated Chaplin enjoyed a modest lifestyle. At the time of his visit to New York the journalist Karl K. Kitchen wrote, 'His only extravagance is a 12-cylinder automobile. He does not even allow himself the luxury of a wife. Jewelry, slow horses and fast company, country homes and *objets d'art* and other expensive fads of the predatory rich do not appeal to this slender young movie actor, who has risen in less than five years from obscurity to the distinction of being the highest-paid employee in the world.'

Chaplin had become 'the highest paid employee in the world' when he left Essanay to sign a contract with Mutual. This had been negotiated by his brother Sydney, who had arrived in America in November 1914. After a brief undistinguished stint as an actor at Keystone, where he had starred in a series of shorts as a character called 'Gussle', Sydney had become Charlie's business manager. Charlie was unhappy with his contract at Essanay, principally because he wrote, directed and starred, but also because the company sold its product in so-called blocks on the strength of the Chaplin films

which were included among the rest in each block. In New York that February, the Chaplin brothers were besieged with offers. Sydney eventually secured the contract with Mutual, signed on 26 February, which guaranteed Charlie $10,000 a week plus $150,000 on signature. Charlie smoothed over the stir caused by this colossal sum, remarking, 'No one realises more than I do that my services may not be worth $100 a week five years from now. I'm simply making hay while the sun shines.'

At Mutual's new Lone Star studio, on the corner of Lillian Way and Eleanor Avenue in the Colegrave district of Los Angeles, Chaplin assumed complete artistic control of his films. Carlyle T. Robinson, Chaplin's press representative from 1917 to 1932, later recalled: '. . . although he was theoretically an employee, his prestige was such that he had the real right to decide ultimately who would work or who would not work at the studio'.

Free of financial worries and in complete command, Chaplin was hitting his stride. In an impressive burst of creativity he made twelve films between May 1916 and October 1917, including *One A.M., The Pawnshop, The Rink, Easy Street* and *The Immigrant*.

One A.M. was a solo performance, once again as a drunk but delivered with infinite brilliance. It is also a display of rapt self-absorption, with Chaplin existing in virtuoso isolation for fifteen minutes, executing every variation on the theme. Behind the solemnly pirouetting figure of the drunk coming home there is another image – a dancer at a bar deliriously contemplating himself in a mirror. *One A.M.* can also be rendered as I AM.

The Pawnshop is another *tour de force* and a superb example of Chaplin's genius for the comedy of trans-

position. In the seedy establishment of the title an alarm clock, presented to Charlie by shabby customer Albert Austin, undergoes successive transformations. The application of a stethoscope turns it into a patient under the probing eyes of a consultant doctor; then it is a piece of priceless porcelain handled with the consummate care of the connoisseur; prised open with a can-opener, its contents seem like a can of putrid sardines; and so on,

until the disembowelled timepiece is reduced to its constituent parts, swept back into the empty case, and returned to a flabbergasted Austin.

In *The Rink* Charlie glided balletically on roller skates. *Easy Street*, a parody of a Victorian morality tale, found the Tramp at his most ingratiating, grabbing the audience's sympathy as a petty-thief-turned-cop, who makes the streets safe for bourgeois promenaders. *The*

ONEY LENT
Secon
Hand
Boug
and
417
MONEY
LENT
EXTENSION LADDER

Immigrant washed the Tramp onto the mean streets of New York, where sentiment is blended with some of Chaplin's most brilliant comedy and a streak of startling social comment. When the huddled mass of immigrants reach New York, a shot of the Statue of Liberty is counterpointed by the sight of immigration officials throwing a rope around the new arrivals as if they were so many cattle.

At Mutual Chaplin assembled a stock company of loyal players and technicians. Among them were the cameraman Roland H. Totheroh – to become known as Rollie – who had first worked with the comedian at Essanay. There was also Eric Campbell, a gentle Scottish giant and Karno veteran, now cast as Charlie's menacing adversary who found his massive buttocks were often the target of the Tramp's well-aimed kicks (and who was memorably subdued with a streetlamp in *Easy Street*). And there was Henry Bergman, a burly

actor of Swedish descent, who first appeared with Chaplin in *The Pawnshop* and who was to become his demanding employer's most slavishly uncritical associate.

Charlie Chaplin's working methods were unique. No matter how big the cast he operated in a kind of isolation, showing every player exactly what he wanted them to do down to the tiniest detail. His was a self-centred artistic universe where only obedient mimicry was permitted. He filmed without a script, shooting in sequence, and often building an entire film around a

LEFT
Chaplin demonstrates the comedy of transposition in The Pawnshop, *released on 2 October 1916 and another film with more of London in it than Los Angeles. Rich in comic invention* The Pawnshop *still delights.*

BELOW
Waiter Eric Campbell presents the Tramp with a bill he cannot pay in The Immigrant, *released on 17 June 1917. Edna and Henry Bergman expect the worst. A masterpiece of artful construction, the film scaled new heights.*

ABOVE
**Charlie and Eric Campbell
menace a helpless golf
ball in** The Idle Class. *Off
the set Chaplin's favourite
sporting pastime was
tennis. His playing days
continued until his late
seventies.*

RIGHT
*Rehearsing an unreleased
First National two-reeler,*
How To Make Movies, *in
1918; (left to right), Tom
Wilson, Chaplin, Henry
Bergman, Edna Purviance,
second cameraman Jack
Wilson (in hat) and Loyal
Underwood.*

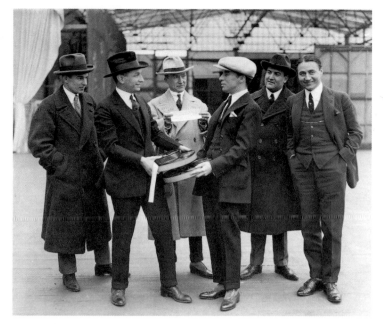

two-reel comedies for them at $150,000 each. Chaplin's output was slowing down dramatically however, and in the next twelve months he produced only three films. *A Dog's Life* (released on 14 April 1918) was made at Chaplin's new studio on La Brea Avenue, and paralleled the life of a winning stray dog named Scraps with two human strays – the Tramp, and a saloon singer (Edna Purviance). *The Bond*, a wartime propaganda short, was distributed without charge throughout the United States in the autumn of 1918. But both of these were over-shadowed by one of Chaplin's greatest successes, *Shoulder Arms*, released on 20 October 1918, just three weeks before the end of the First World War.

Shoulder Arms took the Tramp to the trenches on the Western Front, where he bombarded the wicked Hun with grenades fashioned from foul-smelling Limburger

single idea. Mutual's publicist Terry Ramsaye, later a film historian, wrote: 'Chaplin comedies are not made. They occur . . .' The filmmaker shot individual scenes innumerable times to get them right – an approach considered a prodigal waste by his contemporaries. He was quite prepared to throw out hundreds of feet of extremely funny material, changing his mind and veering up and down blind alleys as he went along. The release print of *The Immigrant*, for example, was edited down from 40,000 feet to 1,800 feet. The thousands of feet of out-takes, numbered in sequence, were stored away on the orders of Sydney Chaplin but, in 1952, when Charlie left America for good, Rollie Totheroh was instructed to destroy them. Fortunately for the history of the cinema, Totheroh made a poor job of it. Years later the film historians Kevin Brownlow and David Gill retrieved hundreds of surviving reels and, by patient jigsaw work, provided TV audiences of our own time with a fascinating insight into their creator's methods in a compilation called *The Unknown Chaplin*.

The enormous success of the Mutual comedies led to Chaplin's celebrated 'million-dollar' contract with First National pictures, signed on 17 June 1917. First National was a production and distribution company which had been formed that year by a number of exhibitors at odds with the block-booking system which Chaplin found so irksome at Essanay. Star power was now the single most important factor in the ever-growing movie business, and First National's first star was to make eight

TOP
Sol Lesser (second left) of First National takes delivery of a film from Chaplin (in cap). Alf Reeves, Chaplin's studio manager, stands between them with a cheque, part of the 'million-dollar' contract.

ABOVE
Charlie in A Dog's Life, a tale of life's strays. In the film he again used the T-shaped Easy Street set, central to his comic vision, whose grimy poverty had a universal quality recognisable from New York to Naples.

cheese and scuttled across no-man's land in a camou-
flage tree in imminent danger of being chopped down
by a huge German infantryman. *Shoulder Arms* was in
part Chaplin's riposte to persistent criticism about his
lack of involvement in the war effort. As early as 22
March 1916, the British *Daily Mail* newspaper had
attacked the star for a clause in his Mutual contract
which barred him from returning to his native land for
war service. In fact, Charlie had volunteered but was
turned down for medical reasons and immediately
thereafter threw himself into energetic campaigning for
War Bonds. (Similar implied slurs on his character were

BELOW
**Mildred Harris, whose
acting career prospered
briefly during her
marriage to Chaplin but
declined after their
divorce. Her last
appearance was as an
extra in** Reap The Wild
Wind **(1942). She died of
pneumonia in 1944.**

FAR LEFT
**The flooded trench in
Shoulder Arms (1918) in
which Charlie, settling
down for a damp night,
jauntily blows out a
candle as it floats by.
Shoulder Arms
demonstrated that
comedy is never so potent
as when it balances on the
edge of tragedy. Chaplin's
achievement was to distill
the horrors of war into a
comedy which was hailed
by men who had endured
life at the front.**

BELOW
**Edna Purviance, Charlie
and Sydney Chaplin in
Shoulder Arms. *Charlie's
heroics included
capturing the Kaiser
(played by Sydney) and job
lots of Huns ('I surrounded
them') but his daring feats
turn out to be nothing
more than a training camp
dream.***

to follow him at intervals for most of his career, and finally drove him to leave his adopted country).

Despite this sporadic sniping from the sidelines, *Shoulder Arms* was a personal, critical and financial triumph for Chaplin. Unfortunately, emotional disaster lay just around the corner. At a party thrown by Sam Goldwyn Chaplin met sixteen-year-old Mildred Harris, a former child actress and film extra. Perhaps the pretty teenager stirred memories of Chaplin's first youthful love, Hetty Kelly. For whatever reason, he married Mildred three days after the release of *Shoulder Arms*. Their union was hurriedly sealed when Mildred announced that she was pregnant. At the wedding, Chaplin was heard to remark that he felt sorry for her. The incompatible couple then moved into a house on DeMille Drive.

As it turned out, Mildred was not pregnant at the time of the wedding but, on 7 July 1919, she bore Charlie a malformed son, christened Norman Spencer Chaplin who, mercifully, died three days later, but whose brief life set the final seal of doom on the already unhappy marriage.

These events probably account for the troubled history of *Sunnyside*, which proceeded in fits and starts between November 1918 and April 1919. *Sunnyside*

located the Tramp in a rural setting, vying with a city slicker for Edna's hand. It contains a strange dream sequence in which Charlie dances through the bosky groves accompanied by nubile wood-nymphs – a nod in the direction of the famous dancer Nijinsky, who had visited the studio (as many others, including assorted Royalty and Winston Churchill would do) and praised Charlie's work as 'balletic'.

Having struggled over *Sunnyside* and hastily assembled *A Day's Pleasure* (released on 15 December 1919), a throwback to earlier slapstick days, Chaplin hit a rich vein of creativity in which he produced an enduring masterpiece, *The Kid*.

For once Chaplin found a foil worthy of his mettle, the bewitching five-year-old Jackie Coogan, whom he had spotted parodying his father's tap-dancing routine at an Annette Kellerman revue. As Chaplin watched, the idea for his first six-reeler sprang into his mind. After trying out little Coogan in the two-reel *A Day's Pleasure*, he cast the boy as the bright-eyed little raga-

FAR LEFT
In pursuit of men of eminence. Chaplin, looking slightly ill at ease, poses with Winston Churchill and his family at Churchill's country home, Chartwell, in September 1931. Shortly afterwards Chaplin met David Lloyd George, later recalling, 'In spite of his interest, I could not help noticing a stifled yawn'.

LEFT
The great Russian dancer Vaslav Nijinsky, who visited Chaplin's studios and complimented Chaplin on the balletic nature of his films. Chaplin's dance in Sunnyside *can be seen as his tribute to Nijinsky's L'Après-midi d'un Faune.*

85

'Six reels of joy'. Never has a film poster been more accurate than this one for **The Kid** (FAR LEFT). Jackie Coogan provided Chaplin with a perfect partner, as Jackie was a mimic of natural genius. No child actor in the history of cinema has produced a performance so touching and un-affected as Coogan in **The Kid**. (LEFT) *Chaplin and Edith Wilson in* **The Kid**. (BELOW) *two faces of Jackie Coogan. By the time Coogan made* **Daddy** *(1923) he was one of Hollywood's top earners. In the same year he moved from First National to MGM in a four-picture million-dollar deal. How-ever, by the mid-1930s Coogan had slipped into obscurity from which he was yanked by a vicious squabble with his mother over the millions he had earned as a child star. When he asked his mother for the money, she told him that under Californian law it was all hers. After a series of costly law suits, there was little left for Jackie. A by-product of this tragedy was the Child Actors Bill, popularly known as 'the Coogan Act', which outlawed such practices.*

muffin. In battered cap and oversized trousers he is raised, lost, and regained (in a heartbreaking dash over the rooftops) by the Tramp. Coogan provided a miniature version of the Tramp's pathos and artfulness, and at times it seems as if the 'Little Fellow', as Charlie called him, is walking hand–in–hand with his adult self.

The Kid cost $500,000 and took eighteen months to film. The final stages of its making were marked by Mildred filing for divorce. Chaplin edited the film in conditions of great secrecy in Salt Lake City and New Jersey, fearful that Mildred might attach the negative as part of the settlement proceedings. *The Kid* finally opened in New York on 6 January 1921, meeting with universal acclaim and turning Coogan into a star in his own right.

Five weeks earlier Charlie Chaplin and his first wife, Mildred Harris, had been divorced.

MODERN TIMES

6

Chaplin had quarrelled bitterly with First National during the making of *The Kid*, but he was not free of his commitment to the company until 1922. In the spring of 1919 however he initiated a new move by becoming a founder member of United Artists.

OVERLEAF
Chaplin confronts the tyranny of the machine age in* Modern Times *(1936). One of his memorable duels was with an automatic feeding device which flings food in every direction but his face, while swabbing his mouth.

ABOVE RIGHT
Early days at United Artists. Left to right, Hiram Abrams, UA's General Manager to 1928, Dennis O'Brian, Mary Pickford and Douglas Fairbanks' attorney, Mary Pickford, her mother Charlotte, Chaplin, Arthur Kelly, Hetty Kelly's brother and Chaplin's representative at UA, Douglas Fairbanks and producer Joseph Schenck.

ABOVE
Filming* City Lights *(1931). Roland Totheroh, the cameraman who worked with Chaplin from 1916 to 1952, recalled that 'the script would develop as it went along . . . we never had a continuity . . . He had a sort of synopsis in his mind but never on paper'.

ABOVE, FAR RIGHT
With Mack Swain in* Pay Day, *a First National film released on 2 April 1922. The film found the Tramp in rare but harassed domesticity, married to Phyllis Allen.

BOTTOM RIGHT
The masked ball scene from* The Idle Class, *a First National film released on 25 September 1921.

T he formation of United Artists (or UA as it became familiarly known) represented a response to the growing corporatism of the movie business by some of its biggest artistic names: Chaplin, D.W. Griffith, Mary Pickford and Douglas Fairbanks. (The stone-faced cowboy star William S. Hart was involved in the early stages but then dropped out). The film companies were planning to put a stop to the huge salaries earned by their stars by a process of merger and the establishment of a mono-poly of distribution outlets. The founder-members of United Artists pre-empted them by forming their own corporation to distribute their own films, whose profits they would retain.

Meanwhile Chaplin was still tied to First National, for whom he made *The Idle Class* (released on 25 September 1921), in which the Tramp savoured the

pleasures of the rich; *Pay Day* (released 2 April 1922), the last of Chaplin's two-reelers in which he played a hen-pecked working man coping with the everyday frustrations of life; and *The Pilgrim* (released in March of 1923), which cast the Tramp in the role of an escaped convict obliged to pose as a priest. *The Pilgrim*'s final scene, in which the Tramp shuffles away to freedom along the border, with one foot in Mexico and the other in the United States, is an image calculated to prompt a range of symbolic interpretations.

Having discharged his contractual obligations to First National, Charlie was free to direct his first film for United Artists. His new independence gave him the opportunity to make a serious dramatic movie, and he embarked on *A Woman of Paris*, which he had first conceived during a visit to the French capital in 1921. A

LEFT AND RIGHT
Chaplin in The Pilgrim, *his last film for First National, released in March 1923. Chaplin played an escaped convict (right) who poses as a priest (left) and becomes reluctant minister to Dead Man's Gulch. In some states religious opinion was so outraged that the film was heavily censored, but it remains one of Chaplin's most smoothly crafted movies and the first for which elements of a written scenario and preparatory notes exist.*

BELOW
A Woman Of Paris, *Chaplin's first venture with United Artists and a sophisticated drama starring Edna Purviance, in her finest screen performance.*

Edna Purviance is massaged by Nellie Bly Baker while Betty Morrisey emotes in A Woman Of Paris. *Baker was not a professional actress but Chaplin's secretary. Subsequently she became a character actress in silent films.*

The snowbound Tramp in The Gold Rush *(1925), the sacking on his right foot substituting for the boot he and Mack Swain have eaten at the height of their hunger pangs. The sequence took three shooting days to film.*

sophisticated and innovatory film for its time, it starred Edna Purviance as a country girl caught between love and money, who becomes the mistress of dapper Parisian man-about-town Adolphe Menjou. Ernst Lubitsch later claimed the film as a great influence on his own sophisticated style. The director allowed himself a cameo appearance as a clumsy porter in a scene at a railway station and, though heavily disguised, he was still instantly recognisable to the sharp-eyed. In his customary fashion Chaplin filmed in sequence over seven months, taking infinite pains over the smallest details. Ninety takes, spread over two days, were needed to capture exactly the effect he required in a small scene in which a bored Edna Purviance throws away a cigarette and refuses to go out.

LEFT
With Mack Swain in The Gold Rush. *Swain played prospector Big Jim McKay, whose raging hunger transforms Charlie into a giant chicken.*

ABOVE
A poster for The Gold Rush. *Lita Grey's pregnancy and subsequent shotgun marriage to Chaplin halted shooting from September 1924 to January 1925.*

CHARLIE CHAPLIN *in* "THE GOLD RUSH"

Premiered on 1 October 1923 at the Criterion Theatre Hollywood, *A Woman of Paris* was greeted with rapturous reviews and brisk business. It fell away quickly at the box office however, closing in Hollywood after only a month. It seemed that audiences wanted Chaplin as the Tramp, not as the trail-blazing director. Nor was the film's release across America helped by bizarre censorship in certain states, which made the motivations of the principal characters all but incomprehensible.

Chaplin buried his feelings about the commercial failure of *A Woman of Paris* in the two years of preparation and shooting he devoted to *The Gold Rush*. In this film the Tramp, alone and adrift in the Frozen North, improvises his sad little cabaret with two forks

and a couple of bread rolls, 'The Dance of the Rolls', and wards off starvation by cooking and eating a boot. Premiered on 26 June 1925 at Grauman's Egyptian Theatre in Los Angeles, *The Gold Rush* was a popular and lucrative triumph, an acknowledged masterpiece still popular today and often shown on TV. It was eventually to gross over $6.5 million against a cost of some $950,000 but, alas, it was also to plunge its creator into another wholly unsuitable marriage.

In March 1924, shortly before locating shooting for *The Gold Rush* began in the snowbound wastes of the Sierra Nevada, Chaplin chose Lillita McMurray, aged 15 years and 10 months, as his new leading lady, changing her name to Lita Grey. Lillita had appeared in *The Kid* as the twelve-year-old 'Angel of Temptation'. Now she provided Chaplin with temptation of another kind and, at the end of September, announced that she was pregnant. On 26 November Charlie married Lita in Guaymas, Mexico, making a fruitless attempt to dodge the press when he tried to sneak back into the United States with his young bride.

The wedding took place three days after the funeral in Hollywood of the director Thomas Ince, whose mysterious death on 19 November, after a cruise aboard the luxury yacht of newspaper tycoon William Randolph Hearst, has never been satisfactorily explained. Ince, one of a party which also included Chaplin, was taken ashore apparently suffering from 'acute indigestion'. He died shortly afterwards at his Hollywood home, the death certificate stating the cause as angina pectoris. However, rumours persisted that Ince's attack of 'indigestion' had been exacerbated somewhat by a bullet fired by Hearst, who had mistaken the unfortunate Ince for Chaplin whom he suspected of having an affair with his own famous mistress, Marion Davies. Certainly Marion was known to be inordinately fond of Charlie at the time, but the ensuing cover-up, and a range of conflicting stories from the principals involved, only served to further muddy the murky waters surrounding an eventful cruise. No official inquest was held into the cause of Ince's death.

LEFT
Chaplin directing The Gold rush *on location at Truckee in the Sierra Nevada*.

INSET
Lita Grey, Chaplin's second wife, in 1946. Their divorce was a very messy business.

Amid these alarums and excursions, Chaplin replaced Lita Grey with a new leading lady for *The Gold Rush*, the eighteen-year-old Georgia Hale. Lita's pregnancy, the perfect excuse, came as something of a relief to her husband. She would not have measured up to the role as an actress, and as a partner she was proving hopelessly incompatible. This change of leading lady did not affect the shooting schedule as Chaplin was filming in

sequence and there had been little call on Lita Grey whose character, the dance-hall girl who becomes the object of the Tramp's fantasies, did not appear until midway through the film. For Georgia Hale (delightful in the part), who had hero-worshipped Chaplin from afar, the experience of working on *The Gold Rush* was rewarding: 'You just knew you were working with a genius. He's the greatest genius of all times for motion

LEFT
Chaplin with equestrienne Merna Kennedy, a childhood friend of Lita Grey, in The Circus *(1928). During filming Chaplin completed over 200 takes inside the lion's cage, and his fear of the very real lions is painfully evident in some scenes. Throughout the year it took to make* The Circus *the Chaplin studio kept an entire circus and its menagerie on the payroll.*

BELOW
Edna Purviance and Chaplin. Edna's weight increased and her confidence diminished in the 1920s, and her last performance was in Josef von Sternberg's ill-fated Woman Of The Sea.

picture business. He was so wonderful to work with. You didn't mind that he told you what to do all the time, every little thing. He was infinitely patient with actors – kind. He knew exactly what to say and what to do to get what he wanted.'

For the genius himself, life on a film set was considerably less complicated than the acrimonious domestic sparring with Lita at their home on Summit Drive. In the autumn of 1925 he began work on a new feature, *The Circus*, shooting of which started on 11 January 1926. The early stages of *The Circus* coincided with Chaplin's unhappy involvement with director Josef von Sternberg who was making *A Woman of the Sea*, starring Edna Purviance. She was by then overweight, nervous and nearing the end of her working life. Chaplin produced the film and, although Sternberg completed it to his own satisfaction, Charlie considered

it too sophisticated for general audiences and it was never released. In 1933, when Charlie was being pressed hard by the Internal Revenue to settle a huge tax bill, *A Woman of the Sea* was destroyed as part of a write-off exercise – a sad end to the beautiful Edna's career.

Eight months into the filming of *The Circus*, Lita left the Chaplin home with the couple's two children, Charles and Sydney. The bitter and prolonged divorce

case which followed attracted lurid headlines and ended in a million-dollar settlement. At the height of his troubles, Chaplin's hair turned white overnight.

On 6 September 1927 work resumed on *The Circus* after an eight-month suspension. Premiered at the Strand Theatre, New York, on 6 January 1928, *The Circus* turned out to be a somewhat scrappy film. It starred the Tramp as a clown enduring a teetering high-wire climax, beset by monkeys and falling trousers, which owed something to Harold Lloyd's 'thrill comedy' and not a little to Chaplin's misfortunes. It was like an anxiety nightmare writ large. Nevertheless, at the first ever Oscar ceremony Chaplin received a special Academy Award for 'versatility and genius in writing, acting, directing and producing *The Circus*'.

At the same ceremony another special award was made to Warners' *The Jazz Singer*, in which Al Jolson uttered the first words ever heard in a feature film, including the legendary phrase, 'You ain't heard nothin' yet!' After the success of the first ever all-talking feature, Warners' *The Lights of New York* (1928), a trade paper commented, 'Thirty per cent of actors are out'. Sound had clearly arrived to stay, but the big stars hung back, reluctant to commit their voices to the crude new microphones and technology.

Of the four founder-members of United Artists – Griffith, Pickford, Fairbanks and Chaplin – only Chaplin was to prove successful in surviving the coming of sound. And, alone among the great stars of the time, he achieved this by simply ignoring the new medium. As late as 1931 he predicted the demise of the talkies, giving them 'three years, that's all'. Audiences could hear Garbo speak, but the Tramp was to remain silent.

In *City Lights*, which opened at the brand-new Los Angeles Theatre on 30 January 1931, Chaplin added only a musical soundtrack (which he composed with Arthur Johnson) to one of his most sentimental films. It tells the tale of a blind flower girl (Virginia Cherrill) whose sight is restored after an operation paid for by the Tramp, whom she believes to be a millionaire. In the final shot she is confronted with her pathetic benefactor, his face illuminated by a nervous smile which combines both hope and apprehension. The critic James Agee considered it to be 'the greatest piece of acting and the highest moment in the movies'. In 1968 Chaplin

TOP LEFT
Merna Kennedy and Chaplin in The Circus. Kennedy subsequently made the transition from silents to sound but retired in 1934 to marry choreographer and director Busby Berkeley. The marriage did not work and they were divorced the following year. Kennedy died of a heart attack, aged 35, in 1944.

BOTTOM LEFT
Greta Garbo, with whom Chaplin planned to make a film about Napoleon and Josephine. The project, along with many others devised for the elusive Swedish star, was never realised. Poignantly, Garbo's last appearance before the cameras, in a screen test for producer Walter Wanger, was made at the Chaplin studios in May 1949.

RIGHT
With Virginia Cherrill in City Lights (1931). Cherrill, a society girl with no acting experience, had a cool working relationship with Chaplin – at one point he considered replacing her with Georgia Hale – but nevertheless produced an affecting performance. She retired in 1933 to marry Cary Grant, one of her five husbands.

described the magic moment, accomplished in a mere seventeen takes on the afternoon of 22 September 1930: 'Sometimes it comes through with a great deal of that magic. I've had that once or twice . . . I had one close-up once, in *City Lights*, just the last scene. One could have gone overboard . . . I was looking more at her (Cherrill) and interested in her, and I detached myself in a way that gives a beautiful sensation. I'm not acting . . . almost apologetic, standing outside myself and looking, studying her reactions, and being slightly embarrassed about it. And it came off. It's a beautiful scene, beautiful; and because it isn't overacted.' Against all odds, *City Lights* was the fourth highest moneymaker of the year.

Chaplin with Douglas Fairbanks on the set of City Lights. *Albert Austin's performance in the film as a burglar marked the last time an old Karno colleague was cast in a Chaplin production.*

LEFT
H.G. Wells, another eminent person pursued by Chaplin, and later rather more amorously by Paulette Goddard, Charlie's third wife. Wells first met Chaplin in England during Charlie's visit in 1921.

RIGHT
Posters for Modern Times, *Chaplin's last silent film. In May 1931 he said 'Dialogue does not have a place in the sort of comedies I make . . . Dialogue always slows action, because action must wait on words'.*

Chaplin had long been lionised by the intelligentsia. On his triumphant return to the place of his birth, London, in 1921, the former street urchin hobnobbed with the likes of H. G. Wells, while the guest of honour at the premiere of *City Lights* was Albert Einstein.

In the early 1930s he developed his own theories on international politics and finance. At the same time, he was toying with several unrealised sound projects, including a version of *Jew Süss*, with himself in the title role. Chaplin was not Jewish though many were convinced he was, and throughout his life he professed great admiration for the Jewish people. He also considered a film about Napoleon – a fellow polymath and autocrat – in which he would play the Emperor and Garbo his consort Josephine. The fragments which survive of these ideas suggest that they were oblique attempts by Chaplin – who had become a voracious reader, devouring books on every possible subject – to tackle the great problems of the day, a task befitting the universal genius which people on all sides kept telling him he had become.

The concrete result was *Modern Times*, which opened in New York on 5 February 1936 and was Chaplin's last silent film – for even he had eventually to bow to the inevitable. With this film he attacked the machine age in inimitable style, pitching the Tramp into the neon-lit world of automation. Nevertheless, at the end of the film he toddles off into the rural never-never land of his Mutual days, accompanied by the Gamine, Paulette Goddard, his latest protegée and third wife whom he married secretly at sea in 1936. Chaplin's only concession to sound in *Modern Times* was a suggestive nonsense song, the first and only time that the Tramp found his voice on the screen.

By the time that Chaplin released his next film, *The Great Dictator*, which had a soundtrack and opened in New York in October 1940, Europe had been plunged into war. That summer American cinema audiences had watched newsreel pictures of Adolf Hitler strutting through Paris after the fall of France, surrounded by his leather-coated generals. Legend has it that *The Great Dictator* was prompted by British film magnate

Alexander Korda's observation of the physical similarity between the Tramp and Adolf Hitler. The resemblance was perhaps more than skin-deep. Both Chaplin and Hitler were auto-didacts of towering ego who channelled their own brand of self-pity into an idealisation of 'the little man'. Chaplin's films can be seen as his own *Mein Kampf*. Ideally, he should have played the destitute young Hitler of his pre-1914 Vienna days rather than the posturing Adenoid Hynkel of the film.

As Chaplin had observed, there was 'a great deal of bad behaviour in the world'. *The Great Dictator* was his

FAR RIGHT
Chaplin with Paulette Goddard, whom he married secretly at sea in 1936. She had met Chaplin four years earlier and co-starred with him in Modern Times as the feisty little orphan on the run from the juvenile officers, a charmingly un-affected performance.

verdict on fascism and his first dialogue film. It was also
the first to start out with a completed script, which ran
to nearly three hundred pages, and also to feature a
well-balanced cast. This last point caused the star some
problems. Previously the splotlight had fallen solely on
the Tramp. As Chaplin explained while making *Modern
Times*, 'We look for some little incident, some vignette
that fixes the other characters. With them the audience
must never be in any doubt. We have to fix them on
sight. Nobody cares about *their* troubles. They stay the
same . . . This is no different from the characters who
surround the "little fellow". *He's* the one we develop.'
Now Chaplin had to contend with such accomplished
actors as Henry Daniell, playing Hynkel's henchman,
Garbitsch, and Jack Oakie, blustering magnificently as
Hynkel's fellow-dictator, the Mussolini-like Benzino
Napaloni.

Chaplin cast himself in the dual role of Hynkel, the
ranting, vainglorious dictator of Tomania, and his
double, a downtrodden little Jewish barber reminiscent

RIGHT
**Chaplin in full flow in The
Great Dictator.** *He never
shot more footage for a
film. Its final running
length of 11,628 feet was
edited from 477,440 feet.*

ABOVE
**A poster for The Great
Dictator,** *Chaplin's
satirical assault on
fascism. Chaplin can fairly
be accused of lapses into
sentimentality and
political naivety, yet he
succeeded, more than any
contemporary film-maker,
in grasping the central
problems of the day and
making biting comment-
aries on them.*

RIGHT
**Chaplin as Adenoid
Hynkel in The Great
Dictator,** *with Jack Oakie
as the bombastic Benzino
Napaloni, dictator of
Bacteria. Chaplin relished
the upstaging battle with
Oakie, an accomplished
comedian. He joked, 'if
you really want to steal a
scene from me, you son-
of-a-bitch, just look
straight into the camera'.*

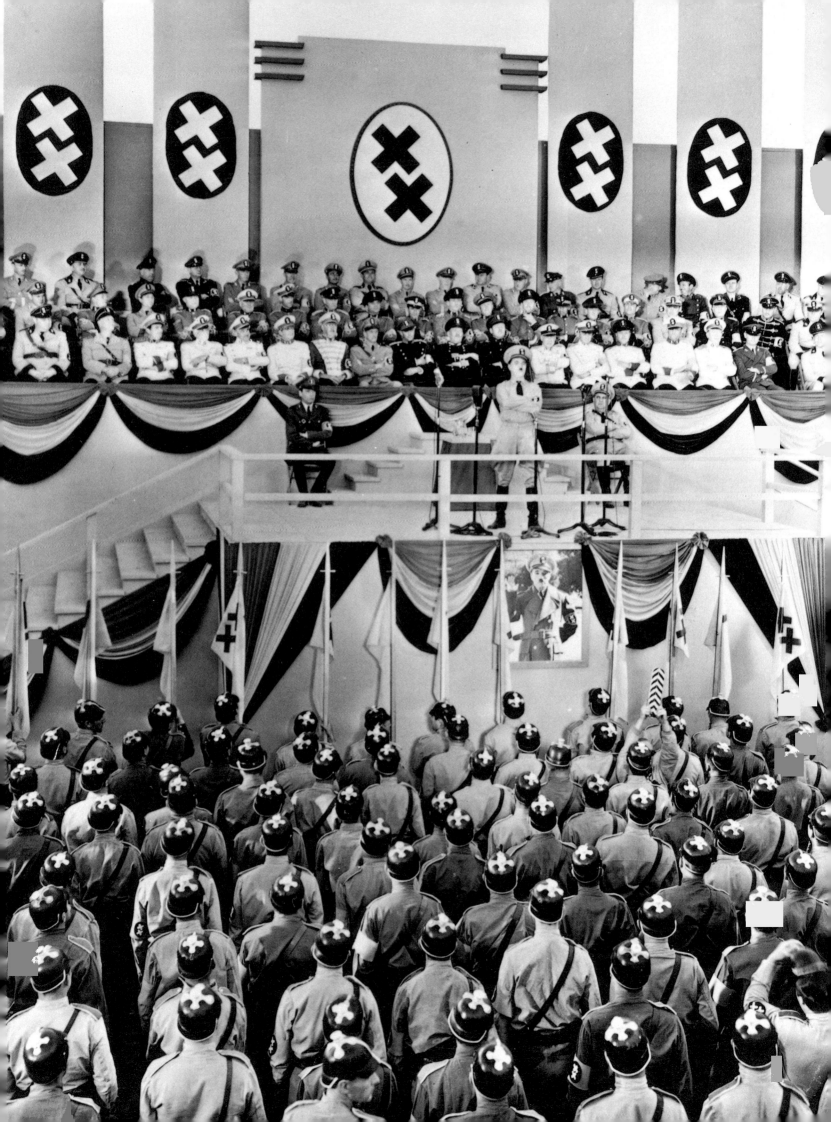

Charlie Chaplin in **THE Great DICTATOR**

HE TALKS...

Produced, written and directed by CHARLES CHAPLIN
with PAULETTE GODDARD
JACK OAKIE · HENRY DANIELL
REGINALD GARDINER · BILLY GILBERT
MAURICE MOSCOVITCH
Released thru United Artists

Chaplin's Adenoid Hynkel, the nightmare vision of a megalomaniac Tramp. But it is his alter ego, the Tramp-like Jewish barber, who delivers the final speech at the end of the film: 'We think too much and feel too little. More than machinery we need humanity. More than cleverness we need kindness and gentleness. Without these qualities life will be violent and all will be lost'. The words still ring true fifty years after Chaplin uttered them.

RIGHT
Paulette Goddard as Hannah in **The Great Dictator.** *Her personal and working relations with Chaplin were now cooler than on* **Modern Times.** *Goddard was now established and experienced and Chaplin, as ever, was an exacting taskmaster. Nevertheless, of all Chaplin's leading ladies Goddard was the one who was most her own woman, lively and appealing, and the one who seems to have nudged Chaplin towards a real warmth for women.*

it the top money-earner of 1941. It opened in London on 16 December 1940, at the height of the Blitz. With death raining from the skies, Chaplin's fellow-countrymen warmly embraced his satire, although there was some critical reservation. The distinguished British critic C.A. Lejeune considered the film 'an uneven work; harsh at some moments, sentimental at others, brilliant, even noble, in many parts'. Perceptively, she added, 'The ghost of every trick that Chaplin has ever played is in the film somewhere. Watching it, your memory ranges back to *The Pilgrim*, *The Kid*, *Shoulder Arms*, even further to the plain, downright days of custard-pie and mallet'. Chaplin never let anything go to waste. As an old home movie in *The Unknown Chaplin* reveals, the origins of the balloon dance – one of the great moments of mime in the cinema – lay in some long-forgotten horseplay on Douglas Fairbanks' lawn in which Charlie, dressed like an Ancient Greek, chases a balloon around in a burlesque of the Isadora Duncan style of dancing.

Later, when the full horror of the Nazi regime was revealed, some felt that *The Great Dictator* was tasteless, laughing in the face of unimaginable barbarism. What remains clear, however, is that it was made as an unequivocal counterblast against the criminal idiocies of fascism, and made at a time when isolationism was still a very powerful force in the United States, leaving the Hollywood majors – with the sole exception of Warner Bros. – unwilling to produce explicitly anti-Nazi films. It was Chaplin's finest hour.

of the Tramp. Inevitably their identities are confused, with the barber becoming a bemused ruler and delivering the long concluding speech to the world, pleading for an end to tyranny. Some of *The Great Dictator*'s impact was muffled by halting construction and descents into sentimentality, but it is richly studded with moments of superb pantomime. There is a scene in the Jewish barber's shop in which Chaplin shaves a customer to the strains of Brahms, and a sinister little ballet in which the idly capering Hynkel toys with a balloon globe of the world, an image both delicate and macabre.

The Great Dictator won Chaplin the New York Critics Award for Best Actor, and its gross of $2 million made

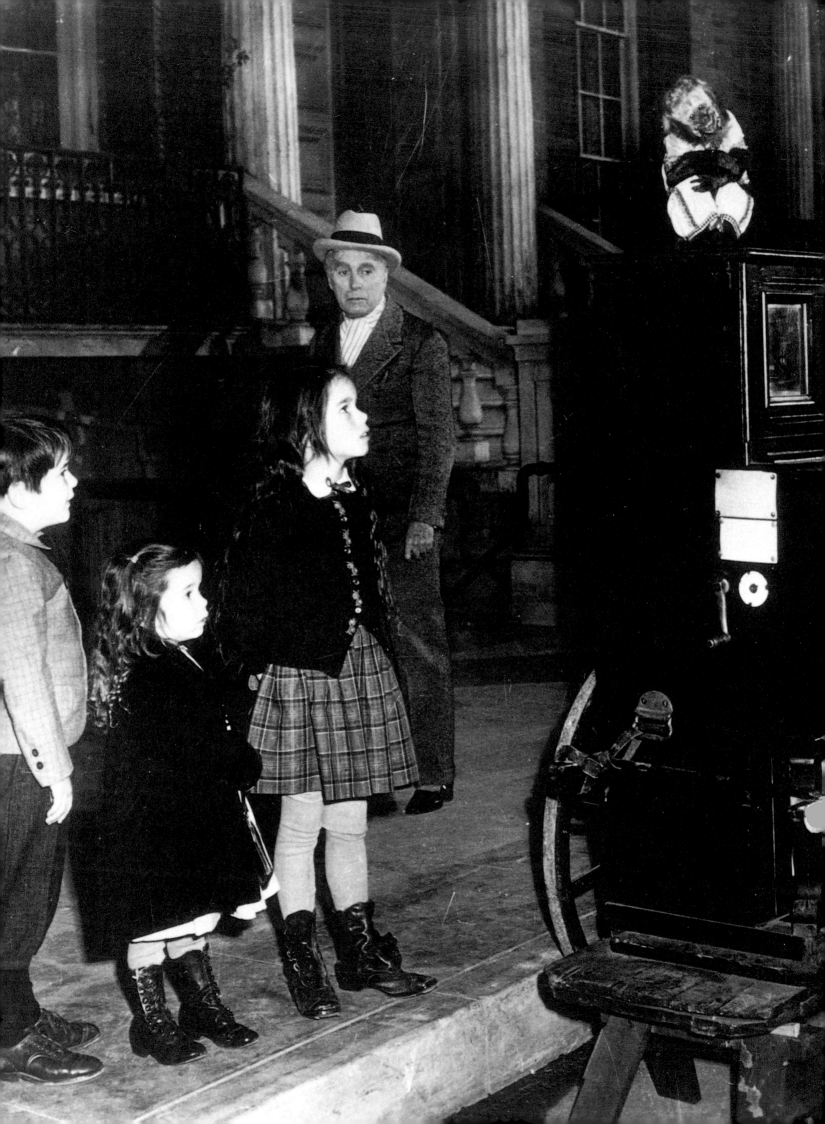

CAUGHT IN THE RAIN

7

After his triumph with *The Great Dictator*, Chaplin slowly drifted away from his audience. He had long been an anachronism in Hollywood, a figure isolated from the mainstream of the big studios and the social life of Tinseltown. Of his original partners in United Artists, Douglas Fairbanks was dead, Mary Pickford increasingly reclusive and D. W. Griffith an embittered alcoholic, observing from the sidelines the industry he had helped to found.

The *Great Dictator*'s extraordinary mixture of creaking construction, sentimental sermonising and inspired mime had underlined Chaplin's technical limitations. This was the inevitable result of the long gaps between his films since *The Circus*, during which time he was overtaken by successive innovations in the business of making motion pictures.

Charlie Chaplin now took the political stage. When the United States entered World War II, he threw himself into championing the cause of the Soviet Union, urging the opening of a second front in a series of speeches which combined impassioned oratory with political naivety in equal measure. The Communist Party of Great Britain printed the final speech from *The Great Dictator* as a special pamphlet. This was hardly likely to endear Chaplin to the American Right, which remained uneasy about the wartime alliance with Stalin's Russia. Nor was his public standing helped by his divorce from his third wife, Paulette Goddard, in 1942 and yet another scandal involving a youthful protegée.

In the summer of 1943 an unhinged young actress named Joan Barry, whom Chaplin had briefly placed under contract a year earlier, announced to the press that she was pregnant by Chaplin. Immediately afterwards, her mother filed a paternity suit. A two-year legal nightmare for Chaplin followed. At the end of it he was found not guilty of violating the Mann Act (transporting a minor across state lines for immoral purposes), but was ruled to be the father of Barry's child in spite of conclusive forensic evidence to the contrary in the form of blood tests. At one point the press were invited to watch as Chaplin was finger printed. Fourteen years later, he inserted a similar scene in *A King in New York*.

Amid the three-ring circus of the Barry court case, Chaplin finally found the ideal partner in Oona O'Neill. She was the eighteen-year-old daughter of the play-

wright Eugene O'Neill, and a young woman of great beauty and character. Although Oona's father disapproved of the match, they were married quietly in South Burbank, California on 16 June 1943. They remained inseparable companions for the rest of

Charlie's life, and Oona bore him eight children (one of whom is the actress Geraldine Chaplin).

Chaplin's misfortunes exposed the fault lines in his relationship with the American public, previously concealed by the overwhelming affection accorded the Tramp. In Thorold Dickinson's phrase, Chaplin remained 'an obstinate English pearl in the oyster of Hollywood'. In his thirty-two years in the United States he had never taken up American citizenship, and this rankled with the conservatives who were now flexing their political muscles in the paranoid post-1945 atmosphere of the Cold War. Chaplin was considered anything but politically sound. The witch-hunt for Communists was already beginning to spread throughout Hollywood, setting in motion a debilitating cycle of fear and betrayal. The sweat stood out on Jack Warner's brow every time he thought of his studio's wartime, pro-Soviet movie, *Mission to Moscow*!

The growing hostility towards Chaplin crystallised around the release, in the spring of 1947, of *Monsieur Verdoux*, perhaps his most intriguing film. Developed from an idea suggested by Orson Welles, *Monsieur*

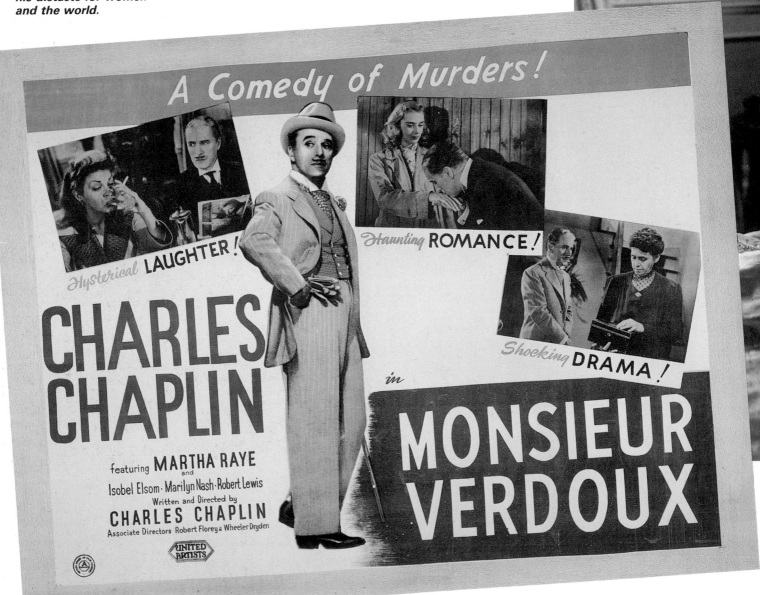

A Comedy of Murders!

Hysterical LAUGHTER! *Haunting* ROMANCE!

Shocking DRAMA!

CHARLES CHAPLIN

featuring MARTHA RAYE
and
Isobel Elsom · Marilyn Nash · Robert Lewis
Written and Directed by
CHARLES CHAPLIN
Associate Directors Robert Florey & Wheeler Dryden

UNITED ARTISTS

in MONSIEUR VERDOUX

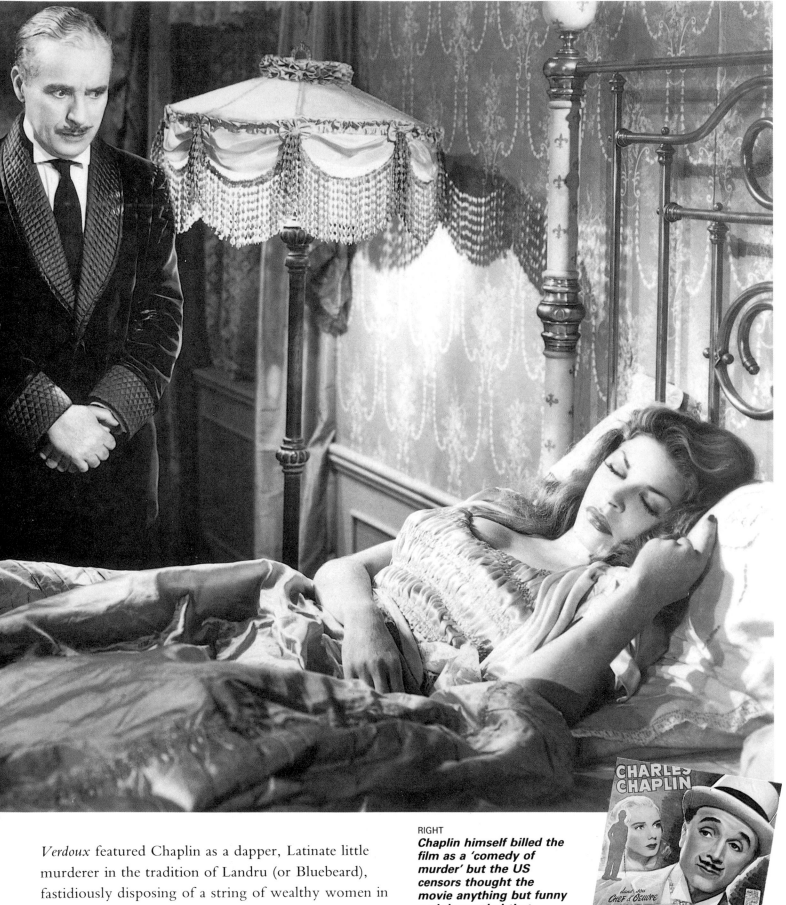

RIGHT
Chaplin himself billed the film as a 'comedy of murder' but the US censors thought the movie anything but funny and demanded that Chaplin make extensive cuts.

CHARLES CHAPLIN

dans son
CHEF d'Oeuvre

MONSIEUR
VERDOUX

MARTHA RAYE
MARILYN NASH
ISOBEL ELSOM
ROBERT LEWIS
Production et Mise en Scène CHARLES CHAPLIN

Verdoux featured Chaplin as a dapper, Latinate little murderer in the tradition of Landru (or Bluebeard), fastidiously disposing of a string of wealthy women in order to support his crippled wife and child. In a chillingly effective image their bodies are burned in an incinerator, whose black smoke rises in the background while Monsieur Verdoux lovingly tends his garden – a cutting metaphor for the agony endured in the Nazi extermination camps while the world looked the other way.

Indeed, in *Monsieur Verdoux* Chaplin has bigger fish to fry than his exquisite little protagonist. Before he is guillotined Verdoux explains that he is merely practising, on a small scale, what is often sanctioned by the state on an infinitely greater scale. Verdoux's point, succinctly made, is that as a businessman he will do anything for profit. He kills rich women for their property; war, and the death of millions of people, is simply bigger business; 'Wars, conflict – it's all business. One murder makes a villain; millions a hero. Numbers sanctify.'

Chaplin had enormous trouble getting *Monsieur Verdoux* past the censors. There was endless wrangling over what the latter deemed to be 'a distasteful flavour of illicit sex, which in our judgement is not good'. In particular they objected to the character played by Marilyn Nash, that of a young prostitute whom Verdoux intends to kill simply to test the efficacy of a new drug, but whom he then spares. More sinister, perhaps, was their disapproving note that 'There are sections of the story in which Verdoux indicts "the System" and impugns the present-day social structure'.

Monsieur Verdoux received its premiere in New York on 11 April 1947 at the Broadway Theatre. Chaplin remembered that there was 'an uneasy atmosphere in the theatre that night, a feeling that the audience had come to prove something'. Hisses mingled with laughter, which to Chaplin seemed like 'a challenging laughter against the hissing faction'. The reviews were mixed. The *New York Herald Tribune* considered the film 'an affront to the intelligence', while the distinguished James Agee thought, 'it is permanent, if any work done during the last twenty years can be considered permanent'. And it was Agee who, spluttering with rage, sprang to Chaplin's defence during a grisly press conference in the Gotham Hotel the day after the premiere. He was provoked to fury when the occasion was exploited by a reactionary hack, James W. Fay, who represented the Catholic War Veterans magazine, and who lambasted Chaplin for his claim that he was 'a citizen of the world' rather than of any one country.

Surprisingly, *Monsieur Verdoux* got off to a brisk start at the box office, but began to falter after a few weeks. With some justification, Chaplin blamed this failure on right-wing pressure groups, claiming that bookings all over America were cancelled after the American Legion threatened to boycott any theatre that showed a Chaplin film. After six weeks its disappointed maker withdrew the film from distribution and did not show it again in the United States for twenty years. He remained convinced that it was 'the cleverest and most brilliant film I have yet made'. It is certainly the most fascinating in the Chaplin canon, full of his underlying misogyny – stemming from broken marriages and paternity suits,

Chaplin and Oona in New York in 1952, the year in which he quit Hollywood for good. His standing with the public was now very low, partly because **of his political beliefs, partly because of successive personal scandals and partly because of his refusal to take US citizenship.**

Waving goodbye to America. The Chaplins on board the liner Queen Elizabeth in September 1952: (left to right) Geraldine, Chaplin, Josephine, Michael, Victoria and Oona. Chaplin was finally to settle in the cloud cuckoo land of Switzerland. Oona died of cancer in September 1991. After her marriage to Chaplin, which so outraged Eugene O'Neill, she never spoke to her father again.

and the mirror image of the Tramp's sentimental vision of women. The savage side of *Monsieur Verdoux*'s satire clearly influenced Robert Hamer when he came to direct another 'comedy of murder' and masterpiece, Ealing's *Kind Hearts and Coronets* in 1949.

While Chaplin was editing *Verdoux*, a US Marshal telephoned him to announce that he was being subpoenaed to appear before the House Un-American Activities Committee to testify on his alleged Communist affiliations. He wired back, 'I am not a Communist; neither have I ever joined any political party or organisation in my life. I am what you call a peacemonger.' Chaplin never appeared before the Committee; had he done so, it might have been the finest performance of his life. The summons, however, was postponed several times and, finally, the Committee let the matter drop.

The FBI however had maintained a bulging dossier on Chaplin for many years and was not going to give up so easily. As David Robinson has pointed out, the Bureau's files on Chaplin tell us more about the rabid anti-Semitism and vindictiveness of the FBI than they do about Chaplin's hazy adoption of socialist beliefs.

But they do provide sad evidence that he had become a marked man after his wartime support for the Soviet Union.

They got him in the end. On 17 September 1952 Charles Chaplin, his wife and their four children sailed from New York in the liner 'Queen Elizabeth' for the British premiere of what turned out to be the last film he made in America, *Limelight*. The ship had been at sea for only a few hours when the American Attorney-General, James McGranery, announced that he had ordered an inquiry as to whether Chaplin should be allowed to re-enter the United States. Two weeks later, the subject of this inquiry was charged with being a member of the Communist Party and making statements which displayed 'a leering, sneering' attitude towards his adopted country. Chaplin had no intention of returning. In April 1953 he handed in his re-entry permit and settled in Switzerland.

Limelight is Chaplin's most deeply personal film. No experience was ever wasted on him, and throughout his career he constantly drew upon his past for inspiration. The frowsty Edwardian streets of Lambeth cast their

Claire Bloom and Chaplin in Limelight *(1952). Bloom later recalled that the young dancer she played was 'some composite young woman, lost to him (Chaplin) in the past'.*

Charles Chaplin Junior with his father in Lime-light. *The elder son by Chaplin's second marriage to Lita Grey, Charles Chaplin Junior had a small role as a pantomime policeman. He later pursued an undistinguished stage and screen career.*

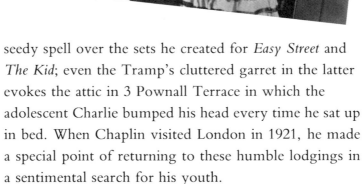

seedy spell over the sets he created for *Easy Street* and *The Kid*; even the Tramp's cluttered garret in the latter evokes the attic in 3 Pownall Terrace in which the adolescent Charlie bumped his head every time he sat up in bed. When Chaplin visited London in 1921, he made a special point of returning to these humble lodgings in a sentimental search for his youth.

In *Limelight* Chaplin slipped back into the vanished world of the music hall in which he grew up. The turn-of-the-century stews of London were his spiritual home, the melodramas and 'penny dreadfuls' read by their inhabitants his original inspiration. When viewed in the context of his life, *Limelight* seems like a many-layered reverie on Chaplin's past, the ground for which he prepared with a remarkable novelised treatment which ran to over 100,000 words.

Calvero, the broken-down comedian he plays in the film, is partly his father but also partly himself, sharing the fear of a live audience which haunted Charlie after

ABOVE
With Claire Bloom in Limelight, *Chaplin's most deeply personal film, peopled with the ghosts of his childhood and music-hall youth.*

RIGHT
Chaplin with Claire Bloom *while she was appearing in a stage production of* **Romeo and Juliet.** *Her autobiography is entitled* **Limelight And After.**

his first success in the movies. Claire Bloom's paralysed dancer, Terry – nursed back to health and stardom by Calvero – is the last in a long line of crippled heroines who were displaced versions of Chaplin's tormented mother. (The Chaplin brothers had brought Hannah to the USA in 1921, where they cared for her till her death in 1926). The ghost of Hetty Kelly (who died in 1918 though Charlie didn't know until three years later) also pulses away in the background. Bloom recalled that during costume tests, 'I quickly realised, even then, that some composite young woman, lost to him in the past, was what he wanted me to bring to life'.

The routines which Calvero plays to an eerie silence, as if they were fantasies of success and failure, recreate precisely the styles of the late-Victorian music hall. And one of them – 'I'm an Animal Trainer' – enabled Chaplin to put a flea circus through its paces. He had been vainly trying to accommodate such a sketch in his films since 1919, when he embarked on *The Professor*, a film of which only a tantalising fragment survives.

Names from the past float through *Limelight*. The kindly impressario, Mr Postant (played by Nigel Bruce), pays tribute to William Postance, the stage manager who kept a protective eye on the young Chaplin during the run of *Sherlock Holmes* in 1905. Poignantly, Chaplin's one-time leading lady, Edna Purviance, appears as an extra. But perhaps most poignant of all is the appearance of Buster Keaton, Chaplin's great rival in the 1920s, playing a hapless accompanist disappearing under a slithering tide of sheet music. Keaton was a half-forgotten figure, one of the 'Hollywood waxworks' in Billy Wilder's brilliant *Sunset Boulevard* (1950), but his

LEFT
Chaplin and Buster Keaton in Limelight. *Of Chaplin, Keaton observed, 'In truth it is at work that he is least funny. Then, calm, lucid and watchful, he pursues his love of perfection with the same attention to detail as a collector handling the wings of butterflies'.*

RIGHT
Claire Bloom meets Princess Margaret at the Odeon Cinema in London's Leicester Square for the premiere of Limelight *on 23 October 1952.*

LEFT
Nigel Bruce as the kindly impressario Postant, Claire Bloom as Terry and Sydney Chaplin (Charlie's second son by Lita Grey) as Neville in Limelight. *During the making of the film Sydney and Claire Bloom became romantically attached.*

BELOW LEFT
Chaplin with Mahatma Gandhi, whom he met in London in 1931 when Gandhi was living in the East End. Gandhi had never heard of Chaplin or seen any of his films.

BELOW
The aviator Amy Johnson, Chaplin, Lady Astor and George Bernard Shaw. Chaplin thought that Shaw used his 'piercing intellect to hide his Irish sentiment'.

Chaplin and Oliver Johnston in A King In New York (1957), a bitter attack on McCarthyism and crass American materialism. A botched film, it nonetheless contains some superb moments of vintage Chaplin mime, notably when his exiled monarch attempts to order caviar amid the din of a crowded night club.

genius was still intact, and the story goes that a jealous Chaplin left some of the best of Keaton's moments on the cutting-room floor.

Shot in fifty-five days – a sprint by the old Chaplin standards – *Limelight* was simultaneously premiered in London and New York on 23 October 1952. It is both corny and clumsily shot – Chaplin's method since the silent days had been simply to plonk the camera down in front of the actors – and the sets, designed by Eugene Lourié, seem flimsy and skimped. And yet the film is infused with the genius of a unique sensibility which links us directly through cinema to the long-dead days of music hall.

Like many other intelligent men, Chaplin had agonised during the 1930s and 40s over choosing between capitalism and socialism. In the end he side-stepped the decision by opting for the cloud-cuckoo world of Switzerland, where he established his family in the comfortable acres surrounding the elegant Manoir de Ban at Corsier-sur-Vevey. He had sold his interest in UA and had no intention of returning to America. In Switzerland he concentrated on his family, interminable spells with the tennis pro and his memoirs. They were published in 1964 and display his astonishingly accurate

memory for small personal and financial details, at the same time as being curiously selective: *The Circus*, for example, is not mentioned at all.

There were, however, two more films to come, the first of which was *A King in New York*, filmed at Shepperton studios in England and released in September 1957. A sad companion piece to *The Great Dictator*, *A King in New York* switches the satirical attack from the fascists of the 1930s to the McCarthyites of the 1950s. Casting himself as the exiled King Shahdov, colliding less than happily with American materialism and mania for social conformity, enabled Chaplin to exact a vicarious revenge on the House Un-American Activities Committee by drenching a bunch of fatuous politicians with a fire-hose. There is a telling sub-plot in which a young boy (played by Charlie's own son Michael) is broken by the Committee's insistence that he 'name names', but on the whole the film seems lost in the unspecific social setting into which Chaplin himself had drifted in Switzerland. As David Thomson has observed, he was 'still unable to approach the world on any other than his own terms'. This was fine for the Tramp, indeed it was the whole point of the Tramp, but it now sat uneasily on the well-tailored shoulders of a plump little man, nearing sixty years of age, whose thin, unlocalised voice seemed more like a talking dictionary than that of a real person.

Chaplin's last film was *A Countess from Hong Kong*, whose story he had first drafted while on a long sea cruise to the Far East with Paulette Goddard back in 1936. Originally entitled *Stowaway* and intended as a vehicle for the lovely Paulette, it now starred the even lovelier Sophia Loren as an adventuress taking refuge in the shipboard stateroom of a stuffy diplomat, played by none other than Marlon Brando. Released in January 1967, at the height of the 'Swinging Sixties', *A Countess from Hong Kong* is more like a featherweight comedy of the 1930s. Moreover, on the set nothing had changed

ABOVE
Chaplin rehearses A Countess From Hong Kong *(1967) with Marlon Brando and Sophia Loren. On his right is Sydney Chaplin and opposite sits Jerry Epstein, a close associate from* Limelight *onwards. Chaplin would have liked to play every part himself. Chaplin (right), as a seasick waiter in* A Countess From Hong Kong, *and (far right), with Sophia Loren on the set.*

BELOW
Oona Chaplin. In Chaplin's extended old age, Oona would sit for hours with him, holding his hand and barely exchanging a word. There was deep bond between them that made it possible for Oona, and Oona alone, to share Chaplin's strange solitude, which was the source of his genius.

LEFT
The last official portrait, taken in 1977. Two months after his death Chaplin's body was stolen by a pair of incompetent grave robbers worthy of the Keystone Kops. They were soon caught and the coffin rescued from its hiding place near Lake Geneva.

ABOVE
Hollywood welcomes Chaplin back at the Academy Awards ceremony in April 1972. Temporarily reduced to the status of adoring fans are, (left to right) Jack Nicholson, Johnny Mathis, Jane Fonda and Sammy Davis Junior. Chaplin recalled the ceremony with irony.

since the days of the silents when Chaplin dominated his own lot while faithful stooges hurried behind him at a respectul distance, waiting to do his every bidding. Now noticeably tubby, but with his silver-haired prettiness preserved intact, Chaplin demonstrated every piece of business to an amused Sophia Loren and a dumbfounded Marlon Brando, and then urged them to copy it as best they could. There was huge interest in the film while it was being made, but when it was released bad reviews killed it at the box office and business was desultory. Chaplin indulged himself by playing a small cameo as a seasick steward, stirring memories of the cabin built on rockers for *Shanghaied*. It was the last screen appearance of the man who had once been the screen's most famous figure.

On 16 April 1972 there was a reconciliation with Hollywood – a triumph of Tinseltown's limitless capacity for cosmic humbug – when Chaplin received a special Oscar. He wallowed in the emotion of the event, delivering halting words of thanks but, as ever, charming the audience – this time with an old vaudeville trick with a bowler hat. Two years later in his book *My Life in Pictures*, he made the astringent observation that 'I was touched by the gesture, but there was a certain irony about it somewhere'.

There was a final honour to come. In 1975 Charlie Chaplin, the Lambeth cockney, attended the investiture at Buckingham Palace and left as Sir Charles Chaplin. He was by then in a wheelchair, and when his name was called to receive his knighthood from Queen Elizabeth II, the orchestra struck up the swooningly romantic theme he had composed for *Limelight*.

In the time that remained to him, Chaplin retreated further into the splendid isolation which had been the main theme of his life and work. Only the devoted Oona was able to penetrate that deep solitude.

Charles Chaplin died on Christmas day 1977, over eighty years after the moment when, as a five-year-old boy, he had rescued his faltering mother from the catcalls of the audience by clambering onto the stage and singing a song. The song will never end as long as his films are shown. Chaplin's was a rare genius. In 1968, while talking about *City Lights*, he recalled, 'I had to correct and act and write and produce a film, cut it . . . and I did it all, which very few did in my day, you know. They didn't do it *all*, you see . . .'

In recent years, Chaplin's reputation has tended to suffer by comparison with that of Buster Keaton who came back into critical and popular favour after a period of neglect. Keaton was certainly the greater natural filmmaker of the two, but it was he who paid Chaplin the ultimate tribute: 'At his best, and Chaplin remained at his best for a long time, he was the greatest comedian who ever lived'. Charlie Chaplin had, above all, a great instinct, and his range narrowed as he grew older so that he never reached full artistic maturity. But as he once observed of himself, 'I always feel such a kid among the grown-ups'.

FILMOGRAPHY

*All films were directed by Charlie Chaplin, unless indicated
otherwise in brackets.*

The Keystone Film Company

1914

Making a Living (Henry Lehrman)

Kid's Auto Races at Venice (Henry Lehrman)

Mabel's Strange Predicament (Henry Lehrman and
   Mack Sennett)

Between Showers (Henry Lehrman)

A Film Johnnie (George Nichols)

Tango Tangles (Mack Sennett)

His Favourite Pastime (George Nichols)

Cruel, Cruel Love (George Nichols)

The Star Boarder (George Nichols)

Mabel at the Wheel (Mabel Normand, Mack Sennett)

Twenty Minutes of Love

Caught in a Cabaret (Mabel Normand)

Caught in the Rain

A Busy Day

The Fatal Mallet (Mack Sennett)

Her Friend the Bandit (Unknown)

The Knockout (Charles Avery)

Mabel's Busy Day (Mabel Normand)

Mabel's Married Life

Laughing Gas

The Property Man

The Face on the Bar Room Floor

Recreation

The Masquerader

His New Profession

The Rounders

The New Janitor

Those Love Pangs

Dough and Dynamite

Gentlemen of Nerve

His Musical Career

His Trysting Place

Tillie's Punctured Romance (Mack Sennett)

Getting Acquainted

His Prehistoric Past

The Essanay Film Manufacturing Company

1915

His New Job

A Night Out

The Champion

In the Park

A Jitney Elopement

The Tramp

By The Sea

Work

A Woman

The Bank

Shanghaied

A Night in the Show

1916

Charlie Chaplin's Burlesque on Carmen

The Essanay–Chaplin Revue (Charlie Chaplin and Leo
   White)

[unauthorized release]

1918

Triple Trouble (Charlie Chaplin)

[unauthorized release]

Chase Me Charlie

Lone Star Mutual

1916
The Floorwalker
The Fireman
The Vagabond
The Count
The Pawnshop
Behind the Screen
The Rink

1917
Easy Street
The Cure
The Immigrant
The Adventurer

Chaplin-First National

1918
How To Make Movies
A Dog's Life
The Bond
Shoulder Arms

1919
Sunnyside
A Day's Pleasure

1921
The Kid
The Idle Class

1922
Pay Day
The Professor [Never released]

1923
The Pilgrim

Regent-United Artists

1923
A Woman of Paris

1925
Gold Rush

1927
The Circus

1931
City Lights

1936
Modern Times

1940
The Great Dictator

1946
Monsieur Verdoux

1952
Limelight

Attica-Archway

1957
A King in New York

Universal

1967
A Countess from Hong Kong

Charles Chaplin Film Corporation

1933
A Woman of the Sea [Produced by Charlie Chaplin, the negative was burnt before release]

Roy Film Establishment – United Artists

1959
The Chaplin Revue [Compilation]

Douglas Fairbanks – United Artists

1921
The Nut (Theodore Reed)

Rupert Hughes – Metro Goldwyyn Mayer

1923
Souls for Sale (Rupert Hughes)

Cosmopolitan – Metro Goldwyn Mayer

1928
Show People (King Vidor)

Filmverhuurkantoor 'De Dam' D.V. – Audjeff

1975
The Gentleman Tramp (Richard Patterson)
[Compilation documentary]

INDEX

Abrams, Hiram; *91*
Agee, James; 100, 114
Anderson, G.M.; 65
Arbuckle, Roscoe 'Fatty'; 48, 52, 60
Armstrong, Billy; *34*, 68
Austin, Albert; *40, 71, 75*

Baker, Nelly Bly; *94*
Bank, The (1915); *70*, 71
Barry, Joan; 111
Barrymore, John; 48
Beery, Wallace; 65
Bergman, Henry; *24*, 77, *77*, *78*, 79
Biograph Studios; 47, 48
Bloom, Claire; *116, 117*, 118, *119*
Bond, The (1918); 79
Bow, Clara; 48, *49*
Brando, Marlon; *121*, 121
Bruce, Nigel; 118, *119*
Bushman, Francis X.; 48, 65
Busy Day, A (1914); 69
By The Sea)1915); 68

Campbell, Eric; *52, 75*, 77, *77, 78*
Carmen (DeMille's film); 73
Casey's Court Circus Co.; *32, 38*
Caught in the Rain (1914); 62
Champion, The (1915); *30*
Chaney, Lon; 48
Chaplin, Annette Emily; *108*
Chaplin, Charles (Jnr); 99, *116*
Chaplin, Charles Senior; 8, 17, *17*, 18, 20, 22, 23, 26
Chaplin, Eugene; *108*
Chaplin, Geraldine; *108*, 111, *115*
Chaplin, Hannah (Charles's mother); *16*, 17, 18, 20, 21, 22, 23, 118
Chaplin, Jane; *108*
Chaplin, Josephine; *108*, 115
Chaplin, Michael; *108*
Chaplin, Minnie; *44*
Chaplin, Norman Spencer; 82
Chaplin, Oona (née O'Neill); *108, 110*, 111, *114, 122*
Chaplin, Sydney (Charles's brother); *20*, 21, 22, 23, 32, 35, *44*, 73, 74, 79, *79, 81*
Chaplin, Sydney (Charles's son); 99, *119, 121*
Chaplin, Victoria; *108, 155*
Charlie Chaplin's Burlesque on Carmen (1916); 73
Cherrill, Virginia; 100, *101*
Churchill, Winston; *85*
Circus, The (1928); *99*, 99–100, *100*, 111, 120
City Lights (1931); *64, 90*, 100–102, *101, 102*, 123
Claire, Ina; *44*
Cold War, The; 112
Conklin, Chester; 51, 54
Coogan, Jackie; *85, 87*

Cooper, Gary; 48
Countess from Hong Kong, A (1967); 71, *121*, 121
Cure, The (1917); *54*

Daniell, Henry; 104
Davenport, Alice; *56*, 62
Davies, Marion; 97, *98*
Day's Pleasure, A (1919); 85
DeMille, Cecil B.; 73
Dickinson, Thorold; 111
Dog's Life, A (1918); *68, 79*, 79
Dressler, Marie; *62, 63*
Dryden, Leo; 20
Durfee, Minta; *56*

Easy Street (1917); 74, 75, *75*, 77, 116
Eight Lancashire Lads, The; *23*, 26
Epstein, Jerry; *121*
Essanay Production Co.; 65, 73, 79

Fairbanks, Douglas; *13, 46*, 47, 90, *91*, 100, *102*, 107, 109
Federal Bureau of Investigation (FBI); 115
Fireman, The (1916); *29*
First National Pictures; 79, 90
Floorwalker, The (1916); 71
Folies Bergère, Paris; 37
Fred Karno Troupe; *27, 40*
Fred Karno's Silent Comedians; 35
Freuler, John R.; 55

Garbo, Greta; 48, 100, *100*, 102
Gillette, William; 32
Gish, Lillian; 48, *49*
Goddard, Paulette; 102, *103, 107, 108, 111*, 111, 121
Gold Rush, The (1925); *10*, 11, *94, 95*, 95–7, *96*, 98
Goldwyn, Sam; 82
Goodwins, Fred; 39
Great Dictator, The (1940); 11, *11*, 102–7, *104, 105, 106, 107*, 111, 120
Griffith, D.W.; *47*, 47, 48, 62, 90, 100, 109

Hale, Georgia; *98*, 98
Hanwell, School, The; 21, 22
Harris, Mildred; *81*, 82, 87
Hart, William S.; 48, 90
Hearst, William Randolph; 97
His Favourite Pastime (1914); 61
His New Job (1915); 66
His Prehistoric Past (1914); *63*, 63
Hitler, Adolph; 103
House of Un-American Activities Committee; 115, 120
How To Make Movies (1918); 78

Idle, Class, The (1921); *78, 90, 91*
Immigrant, The (1917); 74, 77, *77*, 79

In the Park (1915); 66
Ince, Thomas; *48*, 97
Insley, Charles; 71

Jazz Singer, The (1927); 100
Jim, A Romance of Cockayne (Theatre, 1903); 30
Jitney Elopement, A (1915); 68, *69*
Johnston, Oliver; *120*

Karno Company; 73, 77
Karno's Pantomime Co.; *43*
Karno, Fred Jr.; *40*
Karno, Fred; 25, 26, 73
Keaton, Buster; *11*, 11, 48, *118*, 118
Kelly, Arthur; *91*
Kelly, Henrietta; 36, 82, 118
Kennedy, Merna; *99, 100*
Keystone Film Co.; 51, 62, 69, 73
Keystone Kops; 35, 51
Kit Auto Races at Venice, California (1914); 58, *59*, 61, 63
Kid, The (1920); 85–7, *86, 87*, 97, 107, 116
Kind Hearts and Coronets (1949, Ealing); 115
King in New York, A (1957); 111, *120*, 120
Knockout, The (1914); 63
Korda, Alexander; 103

L-KO Production Co.; 73
Laurel, Stan; 37, *37, 40, 43*, 45, 73
Lehrman, Henry; 54, *57*, 73
Leno, Dan; 14, 60
Lights of New York, The (1928); 100
Limelight (1952); *108*, 115–20, *116, 117, 118, 119*, 123
Lloyd, Harold; 48, 100
Lloyd, Marie; 14, *15*, 18
Lone Star Studio (Mutual); 74
Loren, Sophia; *121*, 121
Lubitsch, Ernst; 94

Mabel at the Wheel (1914); *61*, 61
Mabel's Busy Day (1914); 63
Mabel's Strange Predicament (1914); 54, 57, *58*, 60
Making a Living (1914); *57*, 63
Mann Act, The; 111
Marceline; 26
McCoy, Harry; *58*, 61
McMurray, Lillita (Lita Grey); 97, *97, 98*, 99
Menjou, Adolphe; *93, 95*
Mission to Moscow (Warner Bros); 112
Modern Times (1936); 68, *88*, 102, *103*
Monsieur Verdoux (1947); *112*, 112–5, *113*

Morrisey, Betty; *94*
Mumming Birds (Theatre, 1909); 37, 73
Murray, William; *38*
Mussolini, Benito; 104
Mutual Films; 73, 74, 77, 79
My Life in Pictures (Charles Chaplin); 54, 123

New Janitor, The (1914); 62–3
New York Motion Picture Co.; 51
Night in an English Music Hall, A (Theatre, 1912); 46
Night in London Society, A (Theatre, 1910); 41
Night in the Show, A (1915); 71
Night Out, A (1915); *66*, 66
Nijinsky, Vaslav; *85*, 85
Niles Studio California; 66
Normand, Mabel; *48*, 48, 50, *58*, 61, *62, 63*
Norwood School, The; 21, 23

O'Brian, Dennis; *91*
O'Neill, Eugene; 111
Oakie, Jack; *104*, 104
One A.M. (1917); 74

Palmer, Mickey; *40*
Parsons, Louella; 66
Pawnshop, The (1916); 74–5, *76*, 77
Pay Day (1922); *91, 93*
Pickford, Mary; *46, 47*, 48, 90, *91*, 100, 109
Pilgrim, The (1922); *92, 93*, 93, 107
Postance, William; 118
Princess Margaret; *119*
Professor, The (1919); 118
Purviance, Edna; 7, *45*, 66, *67, 68, 68, 69*, 77, *78*, 79, *81, 93, 94, 99*, 99, 118

Raye, Martha; *113*
Reeves, Alf; *43*, 51, 79
Reeves, Amy; *40, 43*
Rendezvous, The (Sydney Chaplin, 1923); 74
Repairs (Theatre, 1906); 32, *34*
Rink, The (1917); 74, 75
Robinson, David; 20, 36, 54, 115

Schenck, Joseph; 91
Sennett, Mack; 35, 48, *48, 50*, 52, 54, 63
Shanghaied (1915); 71, 121
Sherlock Holmes (Theatre, 1903); 30, 32, 118
Shoulder Arms (1918); 79–82, *80, 81*, 107
Spoor, George K.; 65
Sterling, Ford; 51, 57, 60
Sternberg, Joseph von; 99

Sunnyside (1919); 68, *82*, 82–5
Sunset Boulevard (1950, Wilder); 118
Swain, Mack; 51, 60, 62, *91*, *95*
Swanson, Gloria; 48, 66, *98*

The Football Match (Theatre, 1908); 35
Thompson, David; 71, 120
Tilley, Vesta; *14*, 14, 18
Tillie Wakes Up (1917); 63

Tillie's Nightmare (Theatre, 1914); 63
Tillie's Punctured Romance (1916); *62*, 63
Tillie's Tomato Surprise (1915); 63
Totheroth, Roland H.; 77, 79
Tramp, The (1915); *6*, *8*, *21*, *22–3*, *60*, 68
Triple Trouble (1918); 73
Turpin, Ben; 65, *67*

Underwood, Loyal; *78*
United Artists; 90, 93, 100, 109, 120
Unknown Chaplin, The (compilation); 79, 107

Vagabond, The (1916); *45*

Warner Bros; 100, 107
Warner, Jack; 112

Welles, Orson; 112
Wells, H.G.; *102*, 102
White, Leo; *67*, *69*, 71
Wilder, Billy; 118
Woman of Paris, A (1923); *36*, 37, *93*, *93–5*, *94*
Woman of the Sea, A (1926, Sternberg); 99
Woman, A (1915); *69*, 69
Work (1915); 68, 71